# The Silence of God
# during the Passion

*The Silence of God during the Passion* is translated from the French published by Éditions Olivétan as *Le silence de Dieu pendant la Passion*.

In the same collection of translations:

*Repentance—Good News!*
*Praying the Psalms*
*Spiritual Maladies*
*The Tenderness of God*
*Becoming a Disciple*
*From Darkness to Light*

# The Silence of God during the Passion

Daniel Bourguet

Foreword by Bob Ekblad

CASCADE *Books* · Eugene, Oregon

THE SILENCE OF GOD DURING THE PASSION

Translated from the original French edition.
Copyright © 2000 Éditions Olivétan, Lyon, France.

Cascade Books
An Imprint of Wipf and Stock Publishers
199 W. 8th Ave., Suite 3
Eugene, OR 97401

www.wipfandstock.com

PAPERBACK ISBN: 978-1-4982-8173-7
HARDCOVER ISBN: 978-1-4982-8175-1
EBOOK ISBN: 978-1-4982-8174-4

*Cataloguing-in-Publication data:*

Names: Bourguet, Daniel.

Title: The silence of God during the passion / Daniel Bourguet

Description: Eugene, OR: Cascade Books, 2016 | Includes bibliographical references.

Identifiers: ISBN 978-1-4982-8173-7 (paperback) | ISBN 978-1-4982-8175-1 (hardcover) | ISBN 978-1-4982-8174-4 (ebook)

Subjects: LSCH: Passion narratives (Gospels) | Jesus Christ—Passion

*Classification: BT431 B6 2016 (print) | BT431 (ebook)*

Manufactured in the U.S.A.                                           07/28/16

# Contents

# Translator's Note

IN SOME INSTANCES THERE are idioms in French that are difficult to translate, but that has not generally been the case with this book. Some translator's notes have been added as footnotes, generally as glosses of the French, sometimes of a more explanatory nature; in every instance these notes have been checked with the author. Biblical passages are mostly the translator's version of the French since at times the point would be lost if this were not so; the author chooses freely among French translations.

# Foreword

THE PUBLICATION OF DANIEL Bourguet's books in English is a valuable contribution to the literature of contemplative theology and spirituality that will nourish and inspire the faith of all who read them. Daniel Bourguet, a French Protestant pastor and theologian of the Huguenot tradition, lives as a monk in the mountainous Cévennes region in the South of France. There at his hermitage near Saint-Jean-du-Gard, Daniel maintains a daily rhythm of prayer, worship, Scripture reading, theological reflection, and spiritual accompaniment. All of his books flow out of a life steeped in love of God, Scripture, and the seekers who come to him for spiritual support.

I first met Daniel Bourguet in 1988 when my wife, Gracie, and I moved from rural Central America to study theology at the Institut Protestant de Théologie (IPT), where he taught Old Testament. The IPT is the Église protestante unie de France's[1] denominational graduate school in Montpellier, France.

Prior to our move to France while ministering among impoverished farmers in Honduras in the 1980s, we had come across the writings of Swiss theologian Wilhelm Vischer and French theologian Daniel Lys by way of footnotes in Jacques Ellul's inspiring books. Vischer had written a three-volume work entitled *The Witness of the Old Testament to Christ*, of which only volume 1 is translated into English.[2]

1. Then the Église réformée de France.
2. Wilhelm Vischer, *The Witness of the Old Testament to Christ*, vol. 1, *The*

That book, along with a number of articles and Daniel Lys' brilliant *The Meaning of the Old Testament*,[3] exposed us to a community of Bible scholars who articulated a continuity between the Old and New Testaments that was highly relevant then and now. This connection would ultimately lead me to Bourguet.

We experienced firsthand how a literal reading of the Old Testament in isolation from the New Testament confession that Jesus is both Lord and Christ (Messiah) brings great confusion, division, and even destruction. In rural Honduras churches often distinguish themselves by selective observance of Old Testament laws and use certain Old Testament stories to inspire fear of God as punishing judge. In North America Christians were drawing from the Old Testament to justify the death penalty and US military intervention in Central America and beyond.

Wilhelm Vischer himself had been an active resister of Nazism from his Old Testament teaching post inside Germany. He resisted the misuse of Scripture to justify anti-Semitism, nationalism, and war, insisting on the importance of the Old Testament for Christian faith at a time when it was being dismissed. He was consequently one of the first professors of theology to be pressured to leave his post and eventually depart Nazi Germany before World War II, and served as Karl Barth's pastor in Basel after he too left Germany. After the war, the church in France, having been widely engaged in resistance to Nazism and deeply encouraged by Barth, invited Vischer to be the professor of Old Testament at the IPT in Montpellier.

Ellul, Vischer, Lys and other French theologians were offering deep biblical reflection that led us to look into theological study in France.[4] We wrote the IPT about their graduate program and discov-

---

*Pentateuch*, trans. A. B. Crabtree (London: Lutterworth, 1949).

3. Daniel Lys, *The Meaning of the Old Testament* (Nashville: Abingdon, 1967).

4. We were able to study with pastor and New Testament professor Michel Bouttier, who was also trained by Vischer and published broadly, including a commentary on Ephesians and a number of collections of provocative articles. Elian Cuvillier followed Michel Bouttier and is currently Professor of New Testament at

ered that Vischer had long since retired after training several generations of pastors. His protégée, Daniel Lys, had recently retired but was still available. In Lys' place was his doctoral student Daniel Bourguet, who also had been trained by Vischer. The IPT welcomed us with a generous scholarship and we were soon making plans to learn French and move to Montpellier.

We were eager for help to understand Scripture after being immersed in Bible studies with impoverished farmers in war-torn Honduras. Disillusioned with America after being engaged in resisting US policy in Central America, we felt drawn to reflect from a different context. We reasoned that studying in a Protestant seminary with a history of persecution in a majority Catholic context would prove valuable. We left Tierra Nueva in the hands of local Honduran leaders and moved to Montpellier two months early to study French and began classes in September 1988.

Daniel Bourguet taught us Hebrew and Old Testament in ways that made the language and text come alive. He invited students into his passion and curiosity as we pondered both familiar and difficult passages of Scripture. I remember continually being surprised at how seriously Daniel took every textual critical variant, even seemingly irrelevant ones. He masterfully invited and guided us to both scrutinize and contemplate each variant in its original language until we understood the angle from which ancient interpreters had viewed the text. Daniel modeled an honoring of distinct perspectives as we studied the history of interpretation of each passage. He sought to hold diverse perspectives together whenever possible, yet only embraced what the text actually permitted, exemplifying fine-tuned discernment that inspired us.

Daniel's thorough approach meant he would only take us through a chapter or two per semester. This meant we took entire courses on Genesis 1-2:4, on Abraham's call in Genesis 12:1-4, and on Jeremiah 31, Exodus 1-2, Psalms 1-2 and others. In each of his courses he

the IPT, writing many high quality books and articles.

included relevant rabbinic exegesis, New Testament use of the Old Testament, and the church fathers' interpretations. Daniel imparted his confidence that God speaks good news now as he accompanied us in our reading, making our hearts burn like those of the disciples on the road to Emmaus—and inspiring us to want to do this with others. In alignment with Vischer and Lys he demonstrated through detailed exegesis of Old Testament texts how God's most total revelation in Jesus both fulfills and explains these Scriptures, making them come alive through the Holy Spirit in our lives and diverse contexts.

While living in France every summer Gracie and I traveled from France to Honduras, spending several weeks sharing our learning with Tierra Nueva's Honduran leadership and leading Bible studies in rural villages before returning back for classes in the Fall. We had pursued studies in France with the vision of bringing the best scholarship to the service of the least in a deliberate effort to bridge the divide between the academy and the poor. Our experience of the rare blend of scholarship and pastoral sensitivity, which you will see for yourself in his books, contributed to us feeling called back to the church, into ordained ministry and back to the United States to teach and minister there. I benefited from his being my dissertation supervisor as I continued to integrate regular study into our ministry of accompanying immigrants and inmates as we launched Tierra Nueva in Washington State.

Daniel Bourguet's writings are like high-quality wine extracted from vineyards planted in challenged soil. Born in 1946 in Aumessas, a small village in the Cévennes region of France, Daniel Bourguet grew up in the heartland of Huguenot Protestantism, which issued from the Reformation in the sixteenth century. He pursued studies of theology at the IPT in Montpellier, including study in Germany, Switzerland and at the Ecole Biblique in Jerusalem. In lieu of military service, Daniel served as a teacher in Madagascar. He was ordained as a pastor in the Église réformée de France in 1972, serving parishes from 1973 to 1987. Daniel wrote his doctoral dissertation[5] while serving as

5. See Daniel Bourguet, *Des métaphores de Jérémie*, Paris : J. Gabalda, 1987.

a full-time parish pastor—a common practice in minority Protestant France, where teaching positions are scarce and pastors are in high demand. This practice often proves fruitful for ordinary Christians and theologians alike, deepening reflection and anchoring theologians in the church and world.

During our residential studies in Montpellier from 1988 to 1991, Gracie and I witnessed Daniel's interest in the early monastics and fathers of the Eastern church. In 1991 Daniel became prior of La Fraternité Spirituelle des Veilleurs (Spiritual Fraternity of the Watchpersons) and felt called to be a full-time monk, leaving the IPT in 1995 for a year in a Cistercian monastery in Lyon before moving to his current site in Les Cévennes in 1996.

Joy, simplicity, and mercy are the three pillars of Les Veilleurs, an association of laypeople and pastors founded by French Reformed pastor Wilfred Monod in 1923 (with a Francophone membership of four hundred in 2013). Members of this fellowship commit to pursuing daily rhythms of prayer and Scripture reading, including noontime recitation of the Beatitudes, Friday meditation on the cross, regular engagement with a faith community on Sundays, and spiritual retreats and reading that benefits from universal devotional and monastic practices. Les Veilleurs has served to nourish renewal in France and influenced the founding of communities such as Taizé. Under Daniel Bourguet's leadership Les Veilleurs thrived. As a member of Les Veilleurs I attended many of his annual retreats, witnessing and experiencing the vitality of this movement firsthand.

Daniel Bourguet's teaching and writing since his departure from his professorship at the IPT in 1995 have focused primarily on equipping ordinary Christians to grow spiritually through engaging in devotional practices such as prayer, Scripture reading and contemplation. Other works that will hopefully appear in English include reflections on asceticism, silence, daily prayer and the trinity. All but three of Daniel's twenty-five or so books are based on his spiritual retreats offered to pastors and retreatants with Les Veilleurs. He has offered retreats to

Roman Catholic, Orthodox, and Protestant communities throughout France and Francophone Europe and is widely read and appreciated as a theologian who bridges divergent worlds and nourishes faithful Christian practice in France. Daniel Bourguet made his first and only visit to the United States in 2005, offering a spiritual retreat in Washington State. He accompanied me to Honduras on that same trip just after Hurricane Katrina ravaged the country, teaching Tierra Nueva's leaders and accompanying me as I led Bible studies and ministered in rural communities.

Daniel left his role as prior in 2012 and now continues his daily offices, receives many seekers for personal retreats, and offers occasional retreats where he lives and writes. In alignment with the early monastic commitment to manual labor, Daniel weaves black and white wool tapestries of illustrations of Biblical stories done by pastor and painter Henri Lindegaard. Daniel's unique contribution includes his Trinitarian approach to biblical interpretation wherein he reads Scripture informed by the early church fathers, with special sensitivity to how texts bear witness directly but also indirectly to Jesus, the Father and the Holy Spirit.

Daniel Bourguet models an approach to Scripture and spirituality desperately needed in our times. He reads the Bible with great confidence in God's goodness, discovering through careful reading, prayer, and contemplation insights that feed faith and inspire practice. Daniel's deliberate reading in communion with the church fathers brings the wisdom of the ages to nourish the body of Christ today. His tender love for people who come to him for spiritual support, and the larger church and world inform every page of his writing, inspiring like practice. May you find in this book refreshment, strength, and inspiration for your journey as you are drawn into deeper encounters with God.

Bob Ekblad

Mount Vernon, WA
July 7, 2016

# Introduction

Reader friend, I hope that you will read these pages as a song of love to God; I hope they resonate with you and your love for him.

The book was born of meditation on the accounts of the Passion. These, in themselves, are songs of great beauty, infinitely great beauty, of such beauty that there can be little response other than silent contemplation of the one they celebrate: the Crucified One.

Just as our hearts turn inward and towards this crucified one, he too turns inward unceasingly towards the one he calls "Father"—his Father and ours, this Father who is invisible and ungraspable, far beyond what we can understand, but nevertheless mysteriously present at the heart of the Passion accounts. Yet, this presence is astonishing in that it is entirely silent. You will have noticed this—the Father's silence throughout the Passion—even when he is addressed in each of Jesus' prayers!

At first sight this silence on the Father's part during the Passion has something troubling or even shocking about it since it seems the silence of absence. It may seem troubling, but we need to go beyond this first impression; when we consider it a little more closely, approaching it in prayer, the silence is revealed as extremely rich, of surprising beauty, of such depth of humble love that it turns our ideas upside down, and we become immersed in the silence of contemplation and adoration.

God's silence during the Passion is his silence before men, to be sure, and particularly so in the case of Christ as being perfectly and totally human. But it is not this alone. There is much more; it is also the Father's silence before the Son, which is to say, it is a silence instinct within the inexpressible mystery of the Trinity. It is here that the silence is transfigured. It comes before us as infinitely more profound than the silences of earth. It is a silence beyond words and beyond all silence, a silence of unfathomable depth, that of Trinitarian intimacy. Who am I to speak of this? What could I say? Nothing, except that since in God everything is love—including his silence—it cannot be anything other than a silence of love, the silence of the Father's ineffable love for the Son. Reader friend, I believe that anything that might appear to us as suggesting the least trace of an absence of love in the Father's silence must be discarded as an indication of poor interpretation on our part. To cast doubt upon the Father's love within his silence is in my eyes wrong and to be guarded against. Rather, our place is to be silent and beseech God to give us light as to his silence.

Who then can tell us the truth about the Father's silence towards the Son during the Passion? The Holy Spirit and he alone, the one who alone can sound the depths of the mystery of God; he alone is able to help us open up to the Father's silence and to understand its mystery. We can be thankful that, happily for us, the Holy Spirit brought the evangelists into the mystery of this silence. He enabled them to ponder it and give it full place in their accounts of the Passion, between the lines of their texts and even in the silences, in such a way that their accounts cause us to hear a mysterious song of love, the song of their love for God.

I have needed a lot of time before putting pen to paper, for fear of sullying or misrepresenting the Father's silence during the Passion. If I do now write, beseeching the Spirit to help me, it is simply to invite you to open yourself more to this silence and inhabit it with the song of your love, the song of your silent adoration with which the varying colors of your prayer will mingle.

May the Spirit himself bless us and lead us into the Father's silence, there to contemplate his humble, fathomless love for the Son.

# CHAPTER 1

# Announcing the Passion

Before going up to Jerusalem and treading the path that would lead to the cross, Jesus took great care to prepare his disciples for what would be for them a real tempest, a profound overturning of everything in their faith and their love for their master. The announcement he made of his Passion was so difficult for them to hear and understand that he had to repeat it several times, and then repeat it again. Each time, he speaks with an infinite love which would mould and enable them to enter little by little into this great mystery.

With great tact, delicacy, and reserve, Jesus announces his Passion without a word of reproach or loading of accusations on anyone—not the religious leaders for their malevolence, not the Roman authorities for their negligence, nor indeed the disciples for their failures. He announces his Passion without setting himself forward as either a victim or a martyr, but very simply and self-effacingly behind the somewhat enigmatic figure of the Son of Man.

What of God, his Father, in these announcements? What is said of him? It may seem surprising, but he says nothing—not a word! Jesus does not so much as mention God. He does not even speak the name of his Father. He announces his Passion with a discretion that guards against speaking about the cost to the Father of seeing the death of his Well-Beloved Son. The love of the Father for the Son and of the Son for the Father is so great, so deep and immeasurable, that there is no way, not even for Jesus, to find human words big or profound enough to speak of it. All the same, it is still extraordinary to have said nothing of a moment when this love is so involved, so touched, so bruised by men's folly, so brutalized by the overflow of sin, of this moment when the death of the Son grieves so deeply the heart of the Father. As Jesus takes time to announce his Passion to his disciples he does so with great reserve, shrouding the love of his Father in silence.

Here are the texts where he makes his announcements, as reported by Matthew; they are also found, in substantially the same form, in both Mark and Luke.

> Then Jesus began to say to his disciples that he must go to Jerusalem, suffer greatly at the hands of the elders, the chief priests and the scribes, be put to death, and on the third day be raised. (Matt 16:21; also Mark 8:31 and Luke 9:22)

> The Son of Man will be delivered into the hands of men; they will put him to death and the third day he will be raised. (Matt 17:22–23; also Mark 9:31 and Luke 9:44)

> Behold, we are going up to Jerusalem, and the Son of Man will be delivered over to the chief priests and the scribes; they will condemn him to death and hand him over to the Gentiles to be mocked, scourged and crucified, and the third day he will be raised. (Matt 20:18–19; also Mark 10:33–34 and Luke 18:31–32)

## The Divine Passives

As we see, in these statements Jesus doesn't once use the word "Father," or even "God." At first sight nothing is suggested that would help us understand God's feelings, or that would allow us a glimpse of what he might experience during the Passion of his Son. This is a respectful and delicate silence on Jesus' part, the silence of the Son's infinite tenderness for his Father.

We mustn't be mistaken here, however, because discreetly, with great tact, Jesus gently lifts the veil on the mystery of the Father. He does this apart from words, between the words, in a subtle way which nevertheless would not have escaped the notice of the disciples; it might well pass us by today, because we have lost sight of the particular finesse Israel had in their way of speaking of God. Israel, in fact, was practiced at speaking of God with a respect that would not name him; they would in this way evoke his transcendence, but without reducing it to the level of common words; and they would suggest his holiness without profaning or defiling it with words from impure human lips. I would ask you, reader friend, to forgive the clumsiness of my explanation; however, we need to make explicit the unspoken element concerning the Father, which the disciples would have understood in Jesus' announcements. May the Holy Spirit help me to say what is beyond words and not besmirch the purity of the Name which is above every name.

One of the more common ways for Israel to talk about God without naming him was what Bible specialists these days term the "divine passive." This way of proceeding means using verbs of action in a passive form. This has the advantage of passing in silence over the actual performer of the action stated by the verb.

Before examining the two divine passives Jesus used in announcing his Passion, here is an example from another of Jesus' sayings, also addressed to the disciples, who, as good Jews, would have been familiar with the method. It is the response of Jesus to James and John, who had asked to sit at his right and left hand: "When it comes to who will sit at my right and my left, it is not mine to grant, but it will be given to those for whom it has been prepared" (Mark 10:40). Prepared by whom? Who has prepared these places? The same incident is also reported by Matthew who no doubt wished to avoid any misunderstanding, and specified that it is for "those for whom it has been prepared by my Father" (20:23). We see that Matthew, as a good teacher, shows Jesus explicitly stating something that in Mark is only implied. We can see in this example that it was a practice with Jesus to think of his Father without necessarily naming him; he speaks by allusion, using these divine passives, out of respect for his name as Father.

## "He will be raised"

In each of the three announcements reported by Matthew, Jesus speaks of his resurrection using a passive, which seems to be a divine passive, "He will be raised." Unfortunately, our translators have tended to follow the regrettable pattern of translating this in the active form ("he will rise"), whereas the Greek undoubtedly is passive (*egerthēsetai*, "he will be raised"). I say "unfortunately" because, by replacing the passive with an active, the translation in the end obscures the role of the one who raised Jesus; the Greek phrasing shows us that Jesus endeavors discreetly to turn our attention to someone other than himself, the one who will raise him, but whom, out of respect for his transcendence and holiness, he nevertheless avoids naming.

By whom, then, was Jesus going to be raised? There was no need to state this to the disciples, familiar as they were with the divine passives; they would have immediately understood what Jesus was saying, and the inexpressible name of the true agent of the resurrection of the Son would have registered on their spirits at once. The disciples would have understood, without even saying to themselves the Name of the one whom Jesus spoke to them so often. They would have silently received what Jesus said, and bowed in their heart before the one who would raise their master.

After Easter, Peter erases any doubt when he speaks to the rulers of the people, telling them very clearly, using the same verb but in its active form, "God raised from the dead Jesus Christ of Nazareth, whom you crucified" (Acts 4:10). In his turn, Paul makes it still more explicit when he writes to the Galatians, "God the Father has raised Jesus Christ from the dead" (Gal 1:1).

The name "Father," like that of "God," is so great and so holy that Jesus himself, as he announces his Passion, takes care not to mention it; and this all the more because he knew the way what he was saying would upset and shock his disciples, to the point of causing them almost to blaspheme. Peter does indeed revolt, saying, "Lord, this must never happen to you" (Matt 16:22), to which Jesus forcibly replies, "Get behind me, Satan!" (16:23). In this setting, with its possibility of blasphemy, Jesus deliberately avoids speaking the holy name of his Father.

"The Son will be raised," Jesus announces. We need to reach out with our hearts, my reader friend, and understand that though Jesus may not have spoken the name of his Father, his heart was a sanctuary for that name. My belief is that Jesus wishes to place the name simply and silently into the most recondite corner of our hearts with an invitation to contemplate, with the help of the Holy Spirit, the inexpressible and holy mystery that the Son will be raised by the Father. It is an infinite mystery. It is the work of the Father in the Son's behalf, which only the Spirit can enable us to ponder. It is a work accomplished in the measureless depths of the love of the Trinity.

The resurrection of the Son by the Father—this is the essential action announced by Jesus as the final, crowning outcome of the Passion. Jesus is inscribing this wonderful work in triplicate onto the memories of his disciples, out in a realm beyond words, so that, as the darkness of the Passion thickened around them, its remembrance would stay alive in them, breathed into them by the Holy Spirit. The name of the Father is so far beyond words that Jesus seems to wish to invite his disciples into the Passion as into a divine silence, a silence befitting holy ground.

## The Silence of the Resurrection

What Jesus announced came to pass: the Father raised the Son. To whatever degree possible, reader friend, in order to better understand the attitude of the Father during the Passion, we will try to examine what happened on the night of the Resurrection. To do this, it seems to me that we need to give ourselves a somewhat larger context—the dialogue between the Father and the Son through the course of Jesus' ministry.

At his baptism in Jordan, a voice was heard addressing Jesus in the following words of great love: "You are my beloved Son, upon whom I have set all my affection" (Mark 1:11). As Mark records these words, he sets them within the profound mystery of the transcendence and holiness of God. He tells us that the words Jesus heard were spoken by "a voice from heaven," but doesn't mention the name of the speaker. At no moment during the account of the baptism does Mark use the name either of "God" or that of "Father." Although it is obvious that only the Father could have spoken in this way to the Son, Mark carefully avoids stating this, observing the Father's transcendence and holiness, which are beyond words. Mark adds that heaven was "split open," using a passive construction which could only be a divine passive. Split open by whom? Mark says nothing more out of respect for the holiness of the one who opened heaven, saying, "You are my Son," at the same moment as the Spirit appeared in the form of a dove. Let us enter, as if on our knees, into the holy dialogue whose depth is that of trinitarian love: the Son receiving in silence the words from heaven, accompanied by the fluttering of the wings of the dove, who descends from the Father onto the Son.

On the cross, at the threshold of death, the Son gathers up all his resources of love, and says to his Father these overwhelming words of trust, "Father, into thy hands I commit my spirit" (Luke 23:46). The Son, in his perfect holiness, is worthy to pronounce the inexpressible name of the Father, and the Father receives in silence the words of the crucified, accompanied by the gentle fluttering of the dove, who ascends from the Son to the Father.

As we follow this magnificent dialogue of love between the Father and the Son, we await some new word from the Father during resurrection night. What would the Father say to the Son when he raised him from the dead? We know nothing. The angels said nothing of this when they welcomed the women at the empty tomb, and neither did Jesus to the disciples on the road to Emmaus, or in the upper room. I feel bound to believe that the action of the Father in raising the Son from among the dead was not accompanied by any words, and that silence is the only measure of this amazing act so far beyond words. The Father, in silence, raised the Son from the dead: O, the fathomless and wonderful silence of the Father as he raised the Son! Easter morning shines with the brilliant, silent light of the Father's infinite tenderness towards the Son.

My reader friend, we should stay here, immersed in the mystery of the Father's silence at the resurrection of the Son. The silence of love is so endless that it extends backwards to illumine the silence of the Father during the Passion. The love of the Father for the Son in the light of Easter is the same as during the darkness of the Passion, of the same measureless depth. Though the love of the Father for the Son is veiled in the dark silences of the Passion and in the silent light of Easter morning, it is the same love. The resurrection morning silence of the Father is inseparable from the silence of the Father during the Passion; it includes, prolongs and illuminates it. We need to keep this in mind as we now engage with Christ on the way of the cross. These two silences work in counterpoint as the Holy Spirit weaves his love song through the gospels; together they tell us of the holy and immeasurable love of the Father for the Son.

## A Silence of Humble Tenderness

The resurrection of the Son by the Father is a magnificent demonstration of the almightiness of God over the power of evil—a harbinger announcing future total and final victory over death. The unquestionable power of God is involved here, with everything that the word "power" can evoke. This is undoubtedly the case, and it is power far beyond anything we can imagine; but at the same time, we have also to confess the highly paradoxical nature of God's almighty power, equally full as it is of infinite tenderness.

The Greek verb *egeirō*, which is used by Matthew in the announcements of the Passion, is correctly translated as to raise or revive, but its first meaning is to awaken (as in Matt 8:25). Looked at this way, the resurrection of the Son by the Father, his sovereign victory over death, can be seen in a new light, one which shows us the Father awakening his Son. For the Father to awaken his sleeping Son, a simple touch of the hand suffices, a simple gesture of tenderness beyond words, a simple, silent gesture of infinite delicacy; a caress from the Father is enough to awaken his Son!

Jesus' own actions leads me to think of the resurrection of Christ in this way. To awaken the dead son of the widow at Nain he made a similar gesture, "he touched the bier" (Luke 7:14). Or again, to awaken the little daughter of Jairus steeped in the sleep of death, "he took her by the hand," a gesture whose tenderness is revealed when Jesus adds, with great gentleness, the words, "Little girl, wake up" (Mark 5:41). At Easter, the Father filled the silence of the night with tenderness as he woke his Son.

Already during the Passion, this gentle tenderness occupied the heart of the silent Father. It was the same tenderness that filled his heart when he awoke the Son. We need to guard this thought in our spirits as something to remember when—as we consider the silence of the Father during the Passion—it seems to become too painful. The infinite tenderness of the Father silently surrounds the Son in the darkness of the Passion, before bursting forth in paschal light.

"The Son will be raised," Christ repeats as a refrain to his disciples. It is a joy for us, my reader friend, as much as for the disciples, that we are prepared by Jesus himself as we are about to cross the threshold and enter the accounts of the Passion. If it should be that we feel troubled by the Father's silence as his Son went the way of the cross, then we know that the difficulty will dissipate on Easter morning when we consider the Resurrected One, upright and luminous in the silence of the Father.

The resurrection of Christ in the silence of the Father was not exposed to human view. The Father raised the Son without showing anyone and without human witness. There were witnesses when Jesus raised Jairus' little daughter, and there were others when he raised the widow of Nain's son, but there were none when the Father raised the Son. The resurrection of the Well-Beloved Son by his Father is accomplished in profound intimacy, reflecting the perfect humility of the Father, who performs this act of tenderness as if in secret, hiding himself. A humble Father! What a wonder this humility of the Father is! If the Father so humbly hides himself from us as he awakens his Son from among the dead, we may easily suppose that he is similarly hidden from us, just as humbly, as he accompanies his Son on the way of the cross.

Prepared like this, reader friend, we can properly engage in our contemplation of the Father's mysterious silence during the Passion. May the Holy Spirit—who alone can sound the depths of the mystery of God—reveal to us, if only in part, the humble and silent presence of the Father with the Son during the Passion.

## "He will be delivered into the hands of men"

In the announcements of the Passion there is another divine passive, which we need to examine because, if misunderstood, it can be the cause of offense and revulsion, even of radical rejection of God and blaspheming of him.

The word for "deliver" is used twice in the passive in these texts, but only one of these uses is a divine passive. When we are told that the Son of Man "will be handed over to the chief priests and scribes" (Matt 20:18), Jesus doesn't specify who will do this out of regard for the one thus envisaged, because he was among those he was speaking to. The continuation of the gospel does however make it clear; it was Judas who would hand his master over to the rulers of the people (26:15). So this is not a divine passive.

However, when it says that the Son of Man "will be delivered into the hands of men" (17:22)—that is to say into the hands of all people, to the whole of humanity—by whom will he then be delivered? No other passage in the gospel illuminates this divine passive. Jesus was silent as to the real agent of the verb, so to whom was he alluding? Who was he keeping silent about, and why? Would it be the Father who delivers his Son over to men, to all men? Well, indeed, yes! Nevertheless this is a statement so heavy with meaning that one understands the fine and reserved silence of Christ; the expression truly thrusts us into the very heart of the mystery of the cross. We need to spend a little time on this word "deliver" if we are to understand what at first sight might seem scandalizing.

We retain here the translation "deliver" or "hand over" for the verb *paradidōmi*, conforming as we do so to tradition, but this should be done with great reticence. The word "deliver" is colored or even booby-trapped by its connotation of betrayal, in large part because of Judas, who did "deliver" Jesus to his enemies. In the Greek, however, *paradidōmi* only very secondarily carries the meaning of betrayal; it primarily expresses the idea of entrusting. In fact, the primary meaning is to "transmit" or "remit," which essentially is to say "to transmit as a trust," as for example to transmit a patrimony to one's posterity, authority to a successor, or a tradition to faithful followers. In this way, a man "entrusted his goods to his servants" (Matt 25:14). In the case of a person, the word straightforwardly conveys this sense of entrusting, as to entrust a child to a tutor for instruction. This is how Paul "was entrusted by the brothers to the grace of God" (Acts 15:40). In this light, I believe that when the Son of Man is "delivered" by God over to men, this clearly means that God was entrusting him to men. With God, as we shall see in the parable of the vinedressers, there is no suggestion of betrayal, and it is wounding to him, so it seems to me, to think of him in this way. With God there is only a love so great that he places confidence in those to whom he entrusts his one and only Son, his Well-Beloved. The question that arises out of this, as I see it, is no longer what to make of a God who would betray his Son, but rather if we can sufficiently render thanks to the God who extends such extraordinary confidence towards us, and so honor this confidence.

We should add Paul's point of view, expressed in two ways which we do well to keep apart. First he says, "God spared not his own Son, but delivered him up for us all" (Rom 8:32); and second, "Christ loved us, and gave himself up for us," or, still more intimately, "The Son of God who loved me and gave himself for me" (Gal 2:20).

This is a wonderful double expansion of the theme by Paul, shedding light on the words of Jesus. "To be delivered up to men" is a work common to the Father and the Son: their common desire, their common will, the expression of their perfect harmony, perfect synergy and perfect communion. The whole of the Passion is lit by this, by the light of the Holy Spirit who shines forth from the heart of the Father and the Son—the Father entrusts his Son to humanity, and the Son entrusts himself. This is the wonderful communion at the heart of the Trinity.

Reader friend, I believe that this is what the evangelists wished to convey with the help of the Holy Spirit. Only the Spirit can enable us to enter the depths of God's heart, the depths of the love communion between Father and Son.


## The Devil's Intrusion

"To deliver Jesus." To go a little further into this important expression which recurs throughout the account of the Passion (Judas delivers Jesus to the Sanhedrin, the Sanhedrin deliver Jesus to Pilate, and Pilate delivers him to the crowd), it would be good to look at one last piece of information, given to us in John's gospel early in the account of the washing of feet, which is to say, at the beginning of the Passion account. "During the meal, when the devil had already put into the heart of Judas the thought of betraying/delivering Jesus . . ." (13:2).

We have seen Paul spelling out as complementary actions the Father delivering the Son and the Son delivering/giving himself; but here John shows the Adversary coming to insinuate himself into the unfathomable divine plan, to sow his tares among the wheat. We will stop here on this verse, reader friend, and think about it in its context of the washing of the feet to see what teaching we can draw from it.

"The devil had put (literally thrown) into the heart of Judas . . ." This expression, "to place/put/throw into the heart," is laden with meaning. The expression is altogether unique in the Bible since nowhere else does anyone put anything into the heart of another, not even God. It's an expression which, it seems to me, denotes a violent, intrusive action, stripped and devoid of all love. Clearly, the devil entertains no love at all, not just with regard to Jesus, but towards Judas either. For Luke's part, when he talks about this intrusion, he just bluntly says, "Satan entered into Judas" (22:3).

"To hand over Jesus." This, Paul tells us, is the inexpressible love of God for people. It is into this great love project that the devil comes to introduce himself. By putting the thought of betraying Jesus into the heart of Judas, the devil is doing nothing other than insinuating himself as an intruder into the very affairs of God, as if he were taking the place of the Father, who alone can hand over the Son. To interfere in God's plans is a sign of the greatest pride; indeed, such is the devil— pride without love.

Jesus knows all this. He knows that Judas has in his heart the thought of betraying him, and has known it from the very beginning (John 6:64). He now closes the matter by saying to the disciples during the last supper, "Verily, verily, I tell you that one of you will betray me" (John 13:21). Jesus knows and is "deeply troubled" (13:21), but he does not shrink back, because there is something else he knows, as

John states earlier in the account; "he knew that the Father had committed all things into his hands" (13:3). Jesus knows this; he knows that in committing everything into the hands of the Son, the Father is demonstrating the absolute confidence he has in him. Indeed, the Father places entire confidence in the Son, just as the Son does in the Father. To commit all things into the hands of the Son is also a sign of the immense humility of the Father, who parts with everything, gives everything, entrusts everything. It is a sign of the humble love of the Father for the Son. Then, in the humble trust that the Son has for his Father and in the humble love he has for his disciples, Jesus rises from the table, wraps a towel around his waist and proceeds to wash the feet of everyone, particularly those of Judas.

This is the lowly, humble love that washes the feet of the one about to betray him.

Lowly, humble love. Yes, the humble love of the Lord who washes the feet of his disciple in silence. The heart of one is filled with the thoughts of the Intruder, the heart of the other is full of the love of his Father. Such is the beginning of the account of the Passion.

The Passion is the confrontation between loveless pride and loving, humble trust. We need to enter in silence, pondering Jesus who silently washes the feet of Judas in endless, humble love.

# CHAPTER 2

# The Parable of the Vinedressers

A S WELL AS THE announcements made to the disciples at which we have already looked, there are a number of other passages that point to the Passion, but we can set nearly all of them aside since they don't add anything to our understanding of God's silence. However, there is one last declaration which is passed on to us by each of the first three evangelists (Matt 21:33–46; Mark 12:1–12; Luke 20:9–19); it is a little like a portal, opening onto the way of the cross, a magnificent, poignant, strong and thoughtful text which will help us better approach the mystery of God's attitude to the cross, and helps all the more in that it comes from the lips of Jesus himself. There is no one better than the Son to reveal to us the mystery of the Father in the full extent of his love; he does this in a veiled way since God is described in the parable under the cover of a person, and with anthropomorphic traits. This serves both to distance God as the altogether Other, while also bringing him very close to us. Such is God in his love, a thousand miles from our human understanding and yet infinitely close. His love is so humble that he draws very near.

The parable is told by Jesus a day or so after the feast of Tabernacles—which is to say a few days before his death—at a moment, no doubt, when he judged his hearers sufficiently prepared to receive his words. He understood that the disciples had already taken on board something of the subject matter, though not in very clear way, not at least with regard to what it would reveal of the Father.

Certainly, Jesus tells this parable in the hearing of the disciples, who we know were with him, but he tells the story also and specifically to the religious leaders—to the chief priests and elders, as Matthew tells us (21:23); to these we add the scribes, who appear in both Mark's account (11:27) and Luke's (20:1); and then also "the people" (Luke 20:9).

The audience was composed of people who knew the Old Testament scriptures, which helps us understand that when Jesus used scriptural allusions, he knew that they would be understood. Luke wasn't in any way incorrect to avoid such allusions—he was writing for gentiles who were becoming Christians and knew little of the Old Testament; but for this reason we need to pay more attention to the accounts of Matthew and Mark if we are to grasp the parable in the depth Jesus intended by rooting it in biblical tradition.

The parable was spoken in the temple in Jerusalem (Matt 21:23), and we need to bear this in mind. In this holy place, Jesus would feel the need to be very careful in his way of speaking about God, and that, moreover, is how he proceeds. For this reason, the word "God" is not actually pronounced; at the end of what he says, he speaks of "the Lord," another historic designation for God, though this was not a mention he could avoid since he was quoting a verse from the Scriptures (Ps 118:22–23).

The most important person in the parable is a father, as we discover at the moment he mentions his son, but we should note that the word "father" is nevertheless not used. This father, surely, is none other than God, so it is interesting to observe that Jesus has just the same respect for the word "father" as he has for "God"; he pronounces neither word, as though they belonged to the class of the inexpressible, names above all other names, names which would be defiled by falling on impure ears—such is the infinite respect of Christ for his Father.

## The Song of the Vine _____

For the fine connoisseurs of the scriptures who comprised Jesus' audience, the parable would send them straight back to a celebrated prophecy—the famous "song of the vine," which is found in Isaiah 5. Here is the text in a translation from the Hebrew into which are integrated the Greek phrasings as reprised in the Greek of the gospel.

1. I will sing for my well-beloved
   the song of my well-beloved over his vineyard.
   My well-beloved had a vineyard on a fertile hill.

2. He hedged it around, removed all the stones
   and planted the choicest of vines.
   He built a tower in its midst and a press for the wine.
   Then he awaited its produce of fine, good grapes,
   but all it produced was bad.

3. Now then, you who live in Jerusalem and men of Judah,
   be judges between me and my land!

4. What more could be done for my vineyard
   that has not already been done?
   Why, when I expected her produce of quality grapes,
   has all she produced proved bad?

5. And now I will tell you what I will do to my vineyard.
   I will break down her hedge that she may be ravaged.
   I will open up gaps in her wall
   that she may be trampled underfoot.

6. I will reduce her to ruins; she will not be pruned or hoed.
   Brambles and thorns will flourish
   and I will give my orders to the clouds
   that no rain should fall in this place.

7. The vineyard of the Lord of the universe, this is the house of Israel,

and the people of Judah, the plant which he cherished.
He looked for equity, and, behold! there was crime!
For justice, and, hark! the cries of the victims!

Mark and Matthew, unlike Luke, explicitly preserve the link made by Jesus with the prophetic song, as we see at the beginning of the parable: "a man planted a vineyard, surrounded it with a hedge, built a winepress and erected a tower." Each of these details, none of which has any particular importance for the parable that follows, are drawn from the prophecy in order to touch the hearts of the hearers; they would understand immediately that the man in question is none other than God, and that the vineyard is the people of Israel, bound to God by a wonderful bond of love, a bond celebrated by the prophet as he calls God the "well-beloved," affianced to his people. The vineyard, in fact, in Jewish culture, is a figure of the fiancee (Song 1:6, 14; 2:15; 8:12).

Touched to the heart by the parable, Jesus' audience could not but listen with close attention and real involvement, but also with a certain degree of apprehension, because the song of the prophet becomes a complaint and even a threat, expressing the suffering of a God who regards himself as having been grieved by his people.

This aggrieved God—to whom we are sensitized by the prophet—is the subject of the parable. There is no innovation in Jesus' presentation of a suffering God; he just takes it further.

## "He leased the vineyard to tenants"

The first surprise Jesus has in store for his audience is the arrival on stage of the tenants. In the prophet's song, God is himself the farmer and he cares for his vineyard, like a fiance for his beloved. In the parable, the owner of the vineyard entrusts his property to others, who undoubtedly were expected to care for the vineyard with the same love as the owner. By introducing these new tenants, it was not part of Jesus' intention to disconcert his audience. On the contrary, he actually honors them. They will quickly recognize themselves, as the gospel indeed tells us they do, because they are present among the listeners, that is, they are the chief priests. These are the ones who were supposed to care for the vineyard, as God's representatives.

Then, however, we see that those who were so honored as to be representatives of God turn out to also be the ones who wound him. We see that God, who in the song of the prophet is found to be so grieved, will now appear as grieved afresh. But this time, it is not by the vineyard itself—the people—but by the tenants, who will treat the owner with contempt and mistreat all those he sends to them.

The number of messengers from God differs in the different gospels, but this matters little because the result is the same, worsening into a crescendo of violence. The more servants are sent to the tenants, the more wounds are inflicted upon God's love, his trust, and his hope.

To say that God is a God who hopes is heavily underscored in the words of the prophet, who uses the verb "to hope" three times, and each time with God as its subject (vv. 2, 4, and 7). This stress on God's hope being placed in his people is even further underlined because absolutely nowhere else in the Old Testament is God the subject of this verb. What wonderful good news that God would have this hope in us ... What an honor and what a joy, and all the more in that he is not expecting anything impossible of us; is it really too much to expect that a vineyard might produce grapes? Even that was to be in its own good time! But what a shame it is for us, and what a disappointment to him, when we consider what in fact we do. O Lord our God, God of mercy, have pity on us!

In the parable Jesus doesn't use the word "hope," but he knows the word is alive in the hearts of his listeners; the reality is definitely there, if hidden. It is a grieved God he presents to us, a God who is disappointed, wounded in his hope, with a wound which is re-opened and aggravated by each new attempt against him by the tenants, as each servant is sent.

Even if the word "trust" is not seen in the parable, God's trust is very much present, as it is in the prophet's song. Doesn't the owner have a right to be trusting since he chose people specifically skilled to fulfil the task entrusted them? It is surely a sign of trust that he would leave on a lengthy journey without any disquietude, convinced that his property is in good hands. Again, what extraordinarily good news it is that God would place this trust in us! He does indeed trust; he is not disinterested and does not abandon or forget, but returns at the right time—the harvest time—to receive his just entitlement of the expected fruitage.

But continually, more and more, his hope is disappointed and his confidence broken, not by the vineyard itself, but by the tenants, and each time, with each attempt against him, it goes a little deeper. Lord our God, God of mercy, have pity on us.

A God who is wounded in his love, disappointed in his hope, and whose confidence is dashed—such is the God Jesus describes to us here, this God who is always loving, always trusting, always hopeful, who prepares for one last try.

## "He had a son"

At this point in the parable, Jesus does not yet allude to his Passion; he does nothing but prepare the ground for what we are seeing, but in time he will clearly center on it. We can simply remark, in any case, that if the cross of Christ is not yet pictured before our eyes, the cross of the vineyard owner is clearly shown and is longstanding; the owner/master has been on that path from the day when the first of his servants returned wounded and with empty hands.

The great innovation which Jesus brings to the prophetic song—and which presents itself to us as genuine announcement of the Passion—is the arrival of a new character, unknown in the prophet's song; "the owner had a son," Jesus tells us, of which there is nothing in the song. The owner is therefore a father. Again there is nothing like that in the song, which presents God as a landowner, as a fiance, but certainly not as a father; in fact, there is nothing that would lead you to understand God as a father. (I am thinking here only of the song of the prophet; elsewhere in the Old Testament, the fatherhood of God is a clear reality.) Jesus' innovation here is in accord with the song, but in a discreet way. The landowner surely is a father because he has a son, but as we have seen, the word "father" is not used. In his gospel, John explains that to propose God as one's Father is blasphemy, pure and simple (5:18). In the presence of the chief priests who are listening, Jesus very adroitly does not state the word "father," while he does have the vineyard owner say "my son" (Matt 21:37, Mark 12:6, Luke 20:13).

Mark and Luke specify that the son in question is the son "well-beloved" of the father, which admirably complements the song, where God is presented as the "well-beloved" of the prophet (v. 1) and the vineyard as "well-beloved" of God (v. 7). This very strong bond of love between the prophet, God, and the people is now open to the well-beloved son of the father.

For the disciples, there would not have been the least doubt; the "well-beloved" son is none other than Jesus, the Christ, stated to be this by God himself on the day of his baptism and at the Transfiguration. To underline this identification, Mark and Luke use the adjective "well-beloved" in just these three passages; that is, at the Jordan (Mark 1:11; Luke 3:22), at the Transfiguration (Mark 9:7; Luke 9:35) and here, each time applying it to the word "Son" and so reserving it for Christ. Matthew says the same thing in a less emphatic manner, but it is just as clear.

For the disciples, then, Jesus brings himself into the picture just before he comes to the Passion. This is important for them because here, more than in the other announcements, he presents the link with the Father.

If the disciples recognized Jesus in the son of the parable, would the same be true for the rest of the audience? Beyond a doubt. We should not forget that at this point we are just a few days before the Passion. Already, rumors had been circulating around the country suggesting that Jesus might be the Son of God (John 9:35; 10:36; 11:27).

## "He sent his son"

In the parable, the well-beloved Son of the Father is sent to the vineyard and to the tenants who intend to kill him. It is here that the parable really becomes an announcement of the Passion. In this parable, this is the beginning of the way of the cross for Jesus.

Would this Father—who initially goes away on a long journey and at the proposed time of his return sends his Son to the vineyard without going himself—not be a God who is distant, or indeed absent, during the Passion, leaving his well-beloved son to tread the way of the cross alone? Isn't the absolute silence of God throughout the Passion an indication of this distance or absence? Either way, the question has been posed and poses itself again: where is God at the time of the cross?

The parable is certainly no more than a parable, presenting human figures which can't give us the whole picture about God; nevertheless, I believe it gives us somewhat of an answer, even if it is only a hint.

The psalmist is asked, "Where is this God of yours?" (Ps 42:4, 11). The same could be asked of Christ, but more poignantly, "You, the well-beloved son, where is this Father of yours?" Just one word from Jesus would be enough for this question to be settled and come to nothing, and we do have this word: "The Father is in me and I am in the Father" (John 14:11). Nevertheless, it is quite clear that a statement like this shares nothing with the style of a parable and would be entirely out of place. It would be quite wrong for the son to say to the tenants when he arrives at the vineyard, "I am in my father and my father is in me!" We are reaching beyond the limits of the parable genre here; we simply understand the immense advantage that parables offer by avoiding overly mystical discourse. What a great thing it is that we have the four gospels, three of which give a large place to parables. The fourth, however, makes no use of them, leading instead, in a more deliberate way, into the heart of mystery.

As we look at the question of the distance—estrangement or absence of the father with regard to his vineyard, and hence of God at the time of the Passion—we should note that there is something in Luke's account of the parable that can help us greatly. This help is found in the words he uses to speak about "sending." Where Matthew and Mark use just one word for send (*apostellō*), Luke uses three (*apostellō, exapostellō,* and *pempō*), which is really quite precious to us, even though, unfortunately, our translators have not been very careful.

Matthew and Mark are content with the one word *apostellō* ("to send"), which they use for the sending of the servants (Matt 21:34, 36; Mark 12:2, 4, 5) and of the son (Matt 21:37; Mark 12:6), as well as for the tenants sending back one of the servants (Mark 12:3).

Luke, on the other hand, is much more nuanced, using the word *apostellō* for the sending of the first servant (20:10) and a derivative of this, *exapostellō*, the correct word for "sending back," which is just what the tenants do to the servants (20:10, 11). This shows that Luke is being careful in his choice of verbs and so draws our attention to the use of the third verb, *pempō*, both for the subsequent servants (20: 11, 12), and above all for the son (20:13).

The difference between *apostellō* and *pempō* is important. With its prefix *apo* which means "away from," the verb *apostellō* has the idea of separation, while *pempō*, the dictionary tells us, includes with the idea of sending that of accompaniment. Thus, according to Bailly, *pempō* means to "send," but also to "escort" or "accompany," with the following precise meaning: "to accompany, speaking of the gods accompanying a mortal." This last usage is extremely illuminating if used in reference to God—he accompanies those he sends. This usage has nothing at all to say in a story of a simple landowner sending someone to his tenants. The verb *pempō* chosen by Luke contributes nothing to the surface meaning of the parable as it refers to the human personages;

but the word helps greatly when it comes to understanding the parable's theological meaning. At a human level, the proprietor of the vineyard, as just a man, could not be at once both close to and far from whomever he sends. However, insofar as God is in view, things are different because he could be at once both far away and near. It is in this way that God the Father "sends" his Son on a pathway to the cross—accompanying him. In men's eyes, Jesus is alone, but, mysteriously, his Father accompanies him. This is a wonderful thing to know, and it is extraordinarily illuminating. The Father accompanies the Son and will accompany him all the way to the cross.

These precious shades of meaning are very present in the discourses of Jesus recorded in John's gospel. The verbs *apostellō* and *pempō* are frequently used here by Jesus, not in parables, but in the remainder of his discussions on his being sent by the Father into the world of men and women: *apostellō* (seventeen times) to suggest the way sending supposes a distance between his Father and himself ("the works that I do testify of the Father who sent me," 5:36), and *pempō* to emphasize how the sending maintains their closeness ("The Father who sent me is with me" 8:16, 29). One word could have been used just as well as the other, but I believe that what is in question is not a simple alternating between the two expressions according to the moment, but that we should have the picture of the two words as two elements of a paradox. The sending of the Son by the Father is a mission which, so to speak, sets the Son at a distance without distance. This distance without distance expresses a paradoxical reality, the reality of a communion none of us know because none of us know the bond of love that unites the Father and the Son. This bond is so strong the Son can say, "The Father is in me and I am in the Father" (10:38), without confusion or separation.

To do things properly, we should translate *apostellō* by one word and *pempō* by another, but unfortunately we are rather impoverished at this point and are limited to the one leveling word, "send."

John states at length what Luke only suggests in the parable, but we should not forget some of Jesus' final words to his disciples before the Passion, which are very enlightening: "You will leave me alone, but I am not alone, because the Father is with me" (John 16:32).

## The Presence of Christ Beside Us

It is essential that we pay attention to the difference between *apostellō* and *pempō*, that we receive it by faith and live by it, because it concerns us to the highest degree; it is found in a paradoxical form when we are told, in particular, that Jesus "sends" his disciples. "I send you," he tells us in one place using the *apostellō* denoting distance (Matt 10:16); but he also says "I send you" with the verb *pempō* (John 20:21), on this second occasion towards the end of the gospel, at the moment of a definite separation from him, at the moment when he is about to pass from sight and when the fear of disconnection might invade our heart. "I am sending you" is a lovely thing Jesus says to us, imparting his peace to us as he employs the word *pempō*. The word is there so that, with his peace, we can feel assured that the sending is not done from a distance, but is that of proximity, of accompaniment.

This fits perfectly with the last words spoken by Jesus to his disciples at the end of Matthew's gospel, at the moment he commissions them. He says to them, "I am with you" (28:20), using the same phrase as he had concerning his Father on the eve of the Passion, "He is with me" (16:32).

Will we one day know the same close intimacy as that between the Father and the Son? I certainly believe so, because this intimacy is the object of Christ's prayer for us, "that they may be one in us, as you are in me and I am in you" (John 17:21). It is not without reason, then, that we believe this; our only part is to open our hearts, and say Amen to this prayer. The intimacy asked of the Father for us by the Son will one day be given to us as the fulfilment by the Father of the Son's prayer. It is hard to think of anything more wonderful.

## "They will honor my son"

The owner of the vineyard, then, sends his well-beloved son to the tenants, and underlying this mission, Jesus tells us, is the overarching thought, "they will respect my son."

This thought occupies the heart of the Father throughout the Passion: "they will respect my Son." Our meditation on the accounts of the Passion suddenly becomes quite altered in the light of this thought, this silent deliberation in the Father's heart. Yes, the Father is silent throughout the Passion; he maintains a profound silence, a silence which is enigmatic, demanding, troubling . . . but which Jesus suddenly and magnificently illuminates for us: throughout the Passion until its last moment, this overwhelming thought resonated in the heart of the Father, "they will honor my Son."

To ponder the accounts of the Passion is to allow oneself to be overtaken by this thought which touches us right to the very core, "Father, you think this of us! You really think that we will respect your Son!" Then the tears of repentance may be given to us: "Father, you see what we did with him! Father in your infinite mercy, have pity on us!"

"They will respect my son." It is clear that these words are a thought that takes place in the heart of the vineyard owner. If this man was addressing the words to his son, he would have said, "they will respect you." Had he been speaking to the tenants, he would have said, "you will respect my son." But no, he said, "they will respect my son," so the thought is one he keeps to himself. There is also no doubt that the thought was not a passing one, but one he went over again and again, a constant refrain in his heart. What would this man have done in the absence of his son but repeat again and again this one thought, "they will respect my son . . . ! they will honor my son . . . !"

To now say that this is what was occupying the heart of God the Father raises another big question: how was Jesus so aware of what was in God's heart when God himself had said nothing to anyone? God's thoughts are impenetrable, a thousand miles above our thoughts (Isa 55:8–9; Ps 139:17–18). Who can know the thoughts of God, what the Father was thinking during the Passion—who? "No one knows the Father," Jesus tells us correctly, but continues, "no one, except the Son" (Matt 11:27). That is the point; if Jesus was no more than just another man, his parable would be pure invention, a fable, agreeable no doubt, but an invention all the same. But Jesus is more than just man, and it is because he is at once both man and God—Very God of Very God, the Son of God—that he alone can tell us the truth through this parable, and reveal to us the truth of what is in the heart of his Father.

In telling us this parable on the eve of his Passion, Christ gives us an immense privilege, revealing that the profound silence of the Father as he approaches the cross is inhabited by this secret thought, this thought which is unceasing to the end: "they will respect my Son." This is a startling revelation. We need to listen to it and allow it space to settle inside us as we ponder it with the help of the Holy Spirit; he alone knows what is in the depths of God's heart, and he alone can help us understand what the Father thinks on the subject of his Son. Reader friend, we need to pray. This simple phrase of Jesus in the parable thrusts us deep into the mystery of the cross, into the mystery of the thoughts in God's heart, and into the mystery of our own hearts, which so poorly esteem the Son.

> O heavenly King, Comforter, Spirit of truth,
> you who are everywhere present, filling all things,
> treasure of goodness and giver of life, come and dwell in us;
> purify from every defilement and save our souls, you who are kind!

## A Hope for the Future

"They will respect my Son." This is for the future, a hope for the future. The song of the vineyard, as sung by the prophet, has already told us the great hope God places in us and also how grievously that hope is disappointed. This is exactly what we find in the parable, this incredible and boundless hope of the vineyard owner. The man's hope is not placed in his son but in the tenants—"they will respect my son." To begin to contemplate the Passion, then, is to welcome the look of hope God reposes not on Christ, but on us. It is an immense and foolish hope God has for us: "they will respect my Son." I say "foolish" because we know what eventuated and how the divine hope was literally nailed by us to the cross. What an infinite wound to the heart of the Father!

Father of infinite mercy, Lord our God, have pity on us!

Is it possible that the Father could pardon us for such a wound? Reader friend, I am overcome, confounded. I fall to my knees when I discover that during the Passion, the first to ask pardon of God is the crucified one himself, who raises for us this prayer, "Father, forgive them, they know not what they do."

"They will respect my Son" is a thought that not only fills the heart of the Father, but also the heart of the one who composed the parable—the heart of Jesus himself, the heart of the Son who advances towards the cross, knowing the thoughts of his Father's silence. The Son can press forward in silence, sustained by the hope of his Father: "my Father hopes in them; he expects them to honor me!" The Son allows himself to be borne along by the silent hope of his Father, to which he adheres with all his heart: "they will respect me!"

Lord Jesus, you see what we did to this hope!

Lord Jesus Christ, well-beloved son of the Father, have pity on us!

## A Trust for the Future

"They will respect my Son." The thought of the vineyard owner is full of hope, but also of trust.

> The tenants I send my son to are professional men; they know what the work of the vineyard is. I have expressed trust in them by leasing them my vineyard and in signing the papers; I still have confidence in them. They may have mistreated the servants I sent them; they have lacked respect and gone so far as murder; in spite of everything, I have not sent the police; I still have confidence in them. I will now send them my son; they won't behave towards him as they have with my servants. They may have lacked respect for them, but they will respect him; they were only servants, he is my son. They will respect my son because my son is worthy. They have not respected me, the father, by killing my servants; they have not respected me because I was not present to their sight; but my son, they will respect him when they see him! When they see him they will think again; they will change their behavior, they will respect him. When they see him they will remember the contract we signed. They will respect my son as they respect their own signature. These are men worthy to be called men, worthy in their commitments and true to their word; they will respect themselves!

We use the word "police" here, in accordance with our own vocabulary. Jesus would have said "soldiers," as indeed he did in another parable, describing a similar situation (Matt 22:7). Something lovely here is that the sending of the son is not accompanied by any armed force, or by any external force or pressure, but rather just by humble love; the only presence is that of an exposed and unprotected son, and his only authority is simply that he is a son, invested with the father's love.

"They will respect my son" is a deeply rooted confidence of the owner in the tenants, but the continuation of the parable tells us how this confidence was received and then despised, wounding the owner most deeply. But don't let us insist too much; there is cause here for tears of shame. We are just as much concerned in this parable, announcing as it does the Passion—we know what we did to the Son.

That said, the thoughts of the vineyard owner in the parable are also the thoughts of God. His trust is the same trust that God has in us; and this divine trust is also the heart of Christ. Like his Father, he has trust in us; he considers us worthy of his confidence. "They will respect me," the Son thinks during the Passion!

## Premeditated Murder

Indeed, Christ has confidence in us. This confidence is wonderful but—mad;[1] so, could it be that we should think of Christ as "naïve"? Forgive me, reader friend, but I believe that we should. Should we also consider God naïve? Could it be that the Son is so simple, and the Father as well? Is humankind worthy of such trust? Can we be worthy of it when we think how this parable of Jesus corresponds to the cruel reality? How many of God's servants, how many of those sent by God have been mistreated, mocked, wounded and killed through the long and lamentable history of humankind?

If we consider God to be naïve, it is the same thing, in different words, that Paul says when he writes that "love believes all things, hopes all things . . ." (1 Cor 13:7). God's trust goes far beyond all other trust; it is stronger than and resistant to all the griefs we might inflict upon it. What makes me say this is the parable itself and the words that Jesus puts into the mouths of the tenants at the moment of their conspiracy.

Jesus describes the tenants' conspiracy for us, but I prefer not to spend too long on it. I find it so shameful, causing us, as it does, to look at our own baseness and wickedness. The conspirators foment a premeditated murder, solely for an inheritance, solely for money!

1. Fr. *fou*, mad or foolish. (Trans.)

However, there is one point here we should examine—the words Jesus puts in the mouths of the tenants: "Come, let us kill him!" What they say is reported in this way by Matthew and Mark, but not by Luke, who is happy to abridge it to "Let us kill him!"

This difference between Luke and the first two evangelists indicates simply that as Luke was writing to the gentile Christians, he didn't think it useful to transmit an allusion Jesus was making to an Old Testament text. It was an allusion that the habitues of the temple who were listening would certainly have understood, as did Matthew and Mark, who faithfully preserved it. The allusion was all the easier to understand because it refers to the Pentateuch, and every good Jew knew these writings, often by heart.

"Come, let us kill him." This short phrase is found just once in the Old Testament, specifically in Genesis, in the mouths of certain men at the very moment when they see approaching them a son sent by his father. The situation is astonishingly similar. The son in question, sent by his father, is of course Joseph, sent by Jacob. Sent to whom? To his own brothers! Seeing Joseph coming, the brothers conspire together, saying in particular, "Come, let us kill him!" (Gen 37:20).

The allusion made by Jesus to this episode in his people's history could only be for him a source of great hope, of renewed trust, for the simple reason that the plot against Joseph miscarried, and he was not killed. The plot failed because Joseph's brothers reconsidered, persuaded by one of their number, Reuben, who convinced them not to carry the project through. Good for Reuben, who alone managed to convince and turn his brothers. It just needed one, one alone, to cause the plot to miscarry.

## One is Enough

Jesus knew all this; the story of the patriarchs was well known to him, and could legitimately fill his heart with hope and confidence. One had been enough, and it would be enough if there was just one among the rulers of the people, at the heart of the Sanhedrin, just one who would come to his defense and convince the others. One would have been enough; and there was in fact one man who Jesus knew, who had come to him at night to meet him, and had held an unforgettable conversation with him. This man, a ruler of the people, a Pharisee and member of the Sanhedrin, was named Nicodemus (John 3). From what follows that account, we know that one day Nicodemus had stood up in defense of Jesus before the Sanhedrin (John 7:50–51.). It is true that Nicodemus' advice had not been followed, but he continued as part of the Sanhedrin, so why would he not take up Jesus' defense once more at the moment the conspiracy was becoming increasingly menacing?

We can put forward Nicodemus, but why think only of him? We learn, in fact, that there were other sympathizers, even among the rulers, who believed in Jesus (12:42). Only, of course, John adds this piece of information: "they did not let it be known because of the Pharisees, not wishing to be expelled from the synagogue." The word "fear" may not be used here, but we can feel it. Though Jesus had sympathizers who felt a certain respect for him, they wouldn't make a stand for him out of fear, that terrible fear which muzzles respect and makes it mute.

Nicodemus, or some new potential Rueben-figure, is why Jesus could continue to hope and to have confidence. Everything could turn around; the Father was right, they would finally come to honor the Son. Perhaps some of them might find the courage to conquer their fear, and rise up in his defense.

## Respect

Are people capable of respecting, honoring the Christ, the Son of God? Are we even capable of respect, period? I believe the answer is yes, as we can see by looking closely at the word (*entrepō*) chosen by Jesus in

31

this parable. It is found in exactly the same form in the three gospels, "they will respect" (Matt 21:37; Mark 12:6; Luke 20:13).

The verb used here by Jesus signifies straightforwardly in the middle voice, "respect," but we can also specify that in the primary meaning of the word, in the active voice, it means "to return, to change." The added Greek prefix *en* signifies that the change is internal, an internal turning, which is to say, repentance. A verse from Leviticus is illuminating here; it makes the word "heart" the subject of our verb: "then their uncircumcised heart will turn back" (26:41). The source of respect is in the heart; it is a fruit of repentance. The heart is well able to respect, in the same way as it is fashioned to turn towards God and even to turn back to God and to repent if it has been turned out of the way.

The initial demonstration of respect in the parable is not the respect the tenants should have shown to the son, but the respect the master has for the tenants; likewise, the primary respect is not what we should have for Christ or for God, but the respect God has for us. At the source of our respect for Christ—or for anyone else—lies the respect God has for us. Humans are able to show respect and honor to the degree that they are able to open up and allow themselves to be touched by the respect God has for them.

In the parable, God's respect for us appears in the respect the master has for the tenants, manifest from the outset in the way the master entrusts his vineyard to them in perfect condition. It is a vineyard he has meticulously prepared, surrounding it with a hedge, putting in the wine press, building a watchtower—all the little tasks accomplished thinking of those to whom he was planning to lease it. The lengthy and patient work was all done to not disadvantage the tenants.

The respect of the master for the tenants continues to be seen in that he respects their freedom to meet their obligations with him and to send back his servants. The master respects the tenants without ever capitulating before the hardness of their hearts, without ceasing to send more servants, without ceasing to hope or trust, right up until he sends his last envoy (Mark specifies that the son is "the last" and sent "lastly," v. 6) when there is no one else left to send. The father sends his son, still hoping that the tenants will open their hearts and change freely, solely through the influence of the love which comes to meet them. He will send them his "well-beloved" son, saying to himself, "they will respect him."

Indeed, God absolutely respects us, and his respect towards us is proof of his great love; he hopes beyond hope and continues to trust beyond all trust. His love "hopes everything, believes everything."

## "Perhaps"

"They will respect my son." These words are reported by Matthew and Mark, but when Luke reports them it is with a small nuance, a slight difference which might appear rather inconsequential, but in reality turns out to be very important. In Luke's gospel we find one extra word, which in fact is very rare, only being found the once in the New Testament, and we can count it on our fingers in the Old Testament. It is a word over which we need to pause; *isōs*, "*perhaps* they will respect my son?"

"Perhaps"—the word suddenly opens before us a doorway through which rush uncertainty, approximation, weakening, and even doubt. What if the tenants don't respect the son? What if no one steps in to defuse the plot?

The word tells how fragile hope and trust are, all the while magnificently respecting the liberty granted to the tenants. "They are free to do as seems good to them, provided of course they respect my son. . . . Perhaps they will have some respect? Maybe, at least a little?" The fragility conveyed in this "perhaps" is not suggesting some fragility in God, but in us, who by our behavior subvert the grounds of God's hope and trust.

33

We could easily use our imaginations and pursue this meditation on "perhaps" as we think about Christ. What if no one intervenes during the trial? If Nicodemus, seized with fear or weakness, fails to step in and is simply silent, does it matter? What if he is silent, holding back the words which could change everything?

What good is there, however, in carrying on like this when we know what is going to happen? We know the cruel reality of the Passion, how betrayals, denials, abandonments come to slowly undermine the hope and trust that Jesus might have, not only in the rulers of the people, but even in his own disciples. That is the reality and it rather overturns the "perhaps," and Jesus has to courageously close the parable without veiling the facts or hiding the cruel reality: "they killed him."

This "perhaps" will lead Jesus just about to the end of the hope he places in people, almost to the end of the trust he has, even in his close friends. We understand more easily why Mark describes Jesus on the threshold of the Passion, as he arrives at the mount of Olives "distressed and anguished" (14:33).

"Perhaps"—this word, which opens the floodgates to a swell of feeling which invades the heart, is inserted into the parable in the thoughts of the vineyard owner, in the heart of the father, which is to say in the heart of God. "Perhaps they will respect my Son?" Before entering the heart of Christ, this "perhaps" is already in the heart of his Father, which is why it is so important, and even poignant, at this moment when Jesus is preparing himself to go to the cross. In God's heart, the hope he places in man is already damaged. The trust he has in us is already substantially shaken. How poverty stricken we are, reader friend.

Poverty stricken, indeed. The downward slope on which this "perhaps" forces us to advance is so slippery that we are liable to tremble with anguish and distress. If there is no reverence for the Son, what reverence would there be for the Father? What if no one respects God? Is there any answer? Surely God alone can provide one and we must not try to answer in his place. We can only examine our own hearts. I believe there is nothing for us to do but stop our mouths, fall on our knees with our face to the ground, and pour out all the tears in our heart in a flood of repentance.

## On the Road to Repentance

This "perhaps" in the heart of the vineyard owner is found twice in God's heart in the Old Testament. In Jeremiah's time, God had already done more than just *think* in terms of "perhaps"; he had openly expressed the idea, pronounced it, letting it be clearly understood. Jeremiah was the witness to this. He alone heard this "perhaps" and reported it:

> Stand in the courtyard of the temple and speak to all those who come from the towns of Judah to worship; tell them everything that I command you to say, and don't leave out a single word. Perhaps (*isōs*) they will listen and will turn each one from their evil ways; then I will repent of all the evil I thought to do to them because of the maliciousness of their actions. (26:2–15)

A little further on he says:

> When the house of Judah hear of all the evil that I plan to bring upon them, perhaps (*isōs*) they will turn each one from their evil ways, and then I will pardon their fault and their sin. (36:3)

If, as we have said, respect, reverence is the fruit of repentance, these words of Jeremiah place us in the same sorry state as the parable but they go a little further into our hearts, and open before us some hope. Effectively, the prophecies of Jeremiah direct us towards repentance; as well as "perhaps they will have some respect," they say "perhaps they will return," which is to say, "perhaps they will repent." Everything depends on the attitude of the people, and on their free will, but it is always connected to the strong promise made by God himself, "I will repent" (26:3), "I will forgive" (36:3). This "perhaps," which opens the door to all possibilities, even the most dramatic, above all opens the door to God's heart, the door from which issues his forgiveness, which is always available.

"Then I will repent of all the evil I thought to do them." This promise of God is essential if we are to understand the end of the parable, "he will destroy those tenants." This ending is extremely brutal, but the whole Bible teaches us that the future violence expressed here is not an inevitable fate but just one future possibility, and not some necessary destiny. It is a powerful warning, a threat which has as its objective to lead us to a different outcome—repentance. This repentance is so urgent and vital that the warning must be forcefully brought to bear. "He will destroy those tenants." This threat is addressed to the tenants themselves as a warning cry, an invitation to change their attitude, to think again, to repent while there is still time.

## Repentance

Along the way to the cross is there anyone who will ask forgiveness from God? Is there anyone who will ask for this? This question poses itself as we enter the accounts of the Passion, knowing that the door to God's heart is open and that his forgiveness flows from it as a tender balm.

Perhaps, reader friend, before we take our first step, we can suggest a few faint lights which glimmer during the Passion, but so tentatively that they are quickly extinguished.

You will remember Peter, dear Peter, sinking into denial but recovering himself, or rather being taken hold of, gripped simply by a look from Jesus, a look of love that brought him to tears; they were bitter tears, tears of repentance, but tears which were lost in the thick darkness of the night (Luke 22:61–62).

You will remember the traitor, Judas, who can cause us to feel so much shame, because he so resembles us. Judas was forthrightly on the road to repentance, to the point of saying to the chief priests as he rid himself of the fruits of his betrayal, "I have sinned by handing over innocent blood" (Matt 27:4). These were sincere and fine words of repentance, but were rejected by the chief priests and those who heard them. This rejection pushed Judas towards suicide rather than addressing his repentance directly to God.

Decidedly no, we have to admit there was no one who asked pardon of God. Jesus heads down the road to the cross and walks it to the very end, his heart full of the last words of the parable, "they killed him!" It is a sad reality and one by which none of the tenants were shaken—a sad reality that fulfils the other word, addressed this time to the disciples, "You will leave me alone" (John 16:32).

But you will also remember, reader friend, that in this loneliness, and as he turns towards the Father whose heart is open to men's repentance, it is the Crucified One himself who cries out, "Father, forgive them, they know not what they do." This wonderful prayer of the Son for us opens the door to God's forgiveness.

## What Will the Father Do?

"Perhaps they will respect my son." If, as we all know, nobody would truly honor him, we can now see how very much Jesus was liable to enter the way of the cross disquieted, anguished, and distressed. If nobody, not even a single disciple, had the courage to pursue his reverence for Christ to its conclusion without being vanquished by fear, there is only one remaining question: what of the Father? How will it be with him? Will he at least honor his Son?

These questions might arise for us, even if they are a little irreverent, but for Christ they were not an issue. If his trust and hope in people have come up against the hardness of the human heart, his trust and hope in his Father have never been disappointed. "You will leave me alone, but I am not alone, because the Father is with me," he says as he enters the way of his Passion. If we doubt this, let us follow him along the way to the cross to see just where the truth lies.

We will begin by following him to Gethsemane on the mount of Olives, the hour when he whittles down the circle from those who have some reverence for him to those in whom he can still hope and have confidence. We will go along, first of all in the company of the disciples, then just with Peter, James, and John, and see his three closest friends sink not into fear but slumber! Going a little further, we will find him alone; we see him on his knees, his heart turned towards the only one who truly honors him, the only one in whom he can trust, the only one in whom he can still hope, the only one who now will observe total silence in order to hear his prayer. In this remarkable heart-to-heart the first word to burst forth is "Father . . ." In this one word I believe we can hear, "You, at least, will honor me! In you, truly, I can trust! In you, really, I can hope!"

# CHAPTER 3

# Gethsemane

FROM THE PART OF the Passion narrative that focuses on Jesus in Gethsemane I am going to look only at the aspects that concern the relationship of Christ with his Father. The gospel texts are of great richness, but we will confine ourselves to our project in this book, which is to look at the rapport between the Father and the Son as we try to grasp the place of the Father, to understand his attitude. His silence is so deep it shouts at us, so loud as to be offensive to some, thinking that it is the silence of absence, that it is a night void of his presence. If we think this way, it is a night which we might easily fill with our rebellions against him, and even our blasphemies.

The first point to stress is that for Jesus, his Father is present, and there is no doubt about it. This is why he addresses him in prayer without needing to raise his voice or cry out to attract his attention. For Jesus, his Father is there in secret, but he is silent, as he is in our private chamber when he welcomes our prayer, according to Jesus' own teaching; "But you, when you pray, go into your room, close the door and pray to your Father who hears you in secret" (Matt 6:6). If it is evident to Jesus that the Father is there in our secret places to receive our prayer, it is also clear that he must be there in Gethsemane, silently and invisibly—truly in secret, but incontestably present—so he can hear and welcome prayer.

"Go into your room"; that is to say, apart from others, in solitude. This is what Jesus does, leaving Jerusalem to go up the Mount of

Olives. He goes further and leaves behind almost all the disciples, just keeping three of them with him—the three most intimate, Peter, James and John. Then he does the same by leaving these last three, though inviting them to pray with the others, as Luke tells us (22:40); he goes further apart in order to be alone, "a stone's throw away," as Luke specifies (22:41). There he is, apart in the night and sheltered from view, away even from his closest friends, far enough that no one would hear his prayer or disturb the intimacy he shares with his Father.

The solitude of Jesus at this moment is clearly of his own seeking, his own desire, and his own initiative. He is careful to arrange this solitude for himself; he thirsts for it as he thirsts for God, for God alone, his Father.

## "You will leave me alone"

Nevertheless, this solitude is also the result of the disciples' failing since they fall asleep at just this moment, bringing to pass in a surprising way what Jesus had predicted, "you will leave me alone" (John 16:32). That is indeed what has come to pass, but it means that the solitude is deeper than Jesus had wished. Jesus certainly wished to be alone, but he was counting on the prayer of his disciples—on that marvelous communion of prayer which means that even in one's own private room, or indeed alone on the Mount of Olives, one is not, properly speaking, alone. Communion or fellowship in prayer effectively brings to solitary prayer a mysterious quality of love, with the strength of bonds woven by the Holy Spirit himself. The Holy Spirit is wonderful, weaving these invisible cords of fellowship so that the solitude becomes a warm solitude, so to speak, with the warmth which flows from fellowship, by the grace of the Holy Spirit.

What takes place, then, in Gethsemane is that the disciples, invited to pray, fall asleep. Sleep causes them to desert prayer so entirely that Jesus finds himself radically alone when he prays.

The culmination of adversity is that the only disciple who is not sleeping at this hour is Judas, who is busy putting into place the final details of his Master's arrest! And he had certainly deserted prayer!

## "The Father is with me"

"You will leave me alone," Jesus said, no doubt with a stab of pain to his heart. "But I am not alone," he adds, "because the Father is with me," this wonderful Father who "neither slumbers nor sleeps" (Ps 121:4). The ties of fellowship woven by the Holy Spirit have disappeared in the sands of sleep. It is the hour of the sorrowful disaffection of his friends, certainly, but the Holy Spirit, who neither slumbers nor sleeps, makes this hour into a completely different type of fellowship—an hour of profound intimacy beyond anything we can think, the fathomless intimacy between the Father, the Son and the Holy Spirit. This is why, having checked on his sleeping disciples a first (Mark 14:37) and then a second time (14:40), Jesus returns each time, without delay, to this incomparable and inexpressible intimacy.

If we know anything about Jesus' prayer in Gethsemane, if the gospel writers have been able to provide us with any information about it despite there being no human witness, it is because the information was given them, not by Jesus (except perhaps after the resurrection?) or by the Father, but by the Holy Spirit at the time of writing. I believe this, just as I believe that it is with the help of the Holy Spirit that we can enter into an understanding of this portion of the Passion and what the evangelists have set down in writing. For this reason we ought to pray, and ask the Holy Spirit to help us understand.

> O heavenly King, Comforter, Spirit of truth,
> you who are everywhere present, filling all things,
> treasure of goodness and giver of life, come and dwell in us;
> purify from every defilement, and save our souls, you who are kind!

41

Here we are, in the presence of the Father and the Son with the help of the Holy Spirit, which is to say in the presence of the Most Holy Trinity, in an infinite mystery . . . what could be more impressive? We should conduct ourselves towards this account of Gethsemane as Moses did before the burning bush. The prayer addressed by the Son to the Father in the silence of the Holy Spirit is a true burning bush; we should take off our shoes and prostrate ourselves on the ground if we are to begin to penetrate the heart of all this. Jesus has fallen to his knees in the garden on the Mount of Olives, having separated himself a little from his disciples; why would we not, in turn, do the same in order to enter—if only a little—into the immeasurable mystery of prayer?

Now that we are in the presence of a burning bush, which burns with the fire of the Trinity and is not consumed, we should remember at the same time that we are in the presence of a man who is burning sorrowfully with another fire, a fire "of anguish and distress," in the terms used by Mark to describe Jesus at the moment he sets himself to pray (14:33).

Jesus' attitude as he goes to prayer is described differently by the three evangelists: "he threw himself on the ground," Mark tells us (14:35); "he threw himself on his face," says Matthew (26:39); and, according to Luke (22:41), "he knelt down." These expressions underline Jesus' adoption of an attitude which is plainly that of a man—which is how we ought to receive it—but this detracts nothing from his divinity. The situation casts us headlong into the deep mystery of Christ as fully God and fully man. The prayer of Gethsemane is truly that of the Son in his full divinity addressing his Father; it is also the prayer of a man in his full humanity addressing his Father. Such is Christ here, at once fully God and fully man. What will I be able to tell you about the contents of his prayer? I can do my best to take hold of the human dimension, but the rest is bound to escape me. Woe is me! Please accept, reader friend, that I can do little more than stammer!

# The Vocative,[1] "Father"

"Father," says Jesus. No other person in the Bible addresses God in this way. This is a point about which we need to be very careful. The fatherhood of God was known and confessed by Israel as a truth, at two levels in fact; the first, collectively, in that God was recognized as the Father of the people as a whole, and then also personally since he was recognized, in particular, as the Father of the king. With regard to the collective level we hear the people say to God, "You are our Father" (Isa 63:16), and this is the confession of the people's representatives as well when they say to Jesus himself, "We have one Father, even God" (John 8:41). At the personal level, we hear the king speaking very clearly in a psalm about this connection with God as Father, "He has said 'you are my son.'"

This divine paternity is indeed affirmed in the first place by God himself, both collectively and personally. "Israel is my son," he says, speaking of the people (Exod 4:22); for the rest, God speaks of the king, the descendant of David, in these terms, "I will be for him a Father and he will be for me a son" (2 Sam 7:14). It is noteworthy too that God was looking for just one thing from this king—that he should cry out "You are my Father" (Ps 89:27).

All this is very clear and beautiful. It doesn't, however, prevent there being a limit that no one was able to cross, a limit of which Israel itself was aware, one which God himself seems to have wished maintained; the limit is important, even though it only appears as a shade of meaning, but it is of great weight.

The uncrossed boundary is the line between the attributive, "You are my father," authorized by God, and the direct address (the vocative), "Father," which God never suggested. We read in the Psalm, "He will say to me, 'you are my Father,'" not, "He will say to me, 'Father.'" You may perhaps find this distinction a useless subtlety, but for those

---

1. Addressing a person directly in the second person is the Latin vocative. (Trans.)

around Jesus it was far from that, and more than important. The difference between the two ways of speaking to God marks the limit between a partial intimacy ("you are my Father") and a profound intimacy ("Father!"). This distinction had been grasped by Israel; to cross this boundary, according to the religious leaders of the people, was to consider oneself as being God. It was "to make yourself God," as was said to Jesus ("You who are a man, make yourself God"—John 10:33). To consider oneself as God was to cross the line into blasphemy. To say to God, "You are our Father," was to confess the faith of Israel without blaspheming (Isa 63:16), but to say to him, "Father," was to blaspheme since it was to cross a boundary of intimacy with God which no man was permitted to cross.

Jesus knew all this, and crosses the boundary just the same by saying, "Father!" in his prayer.

## The Trinitarian Mystery

To take oneself for God, to make oneself God, to consider oneself as God, is obviously a blasphemous attitude and full of pride. We must therefore choose: either we say that Jesus is a blasphemer, which would be understandable, or we confess that, if Jesus spoke as he did without blaspheming, it is not because he was "making himself" God but in fact "is" God. Of course, it emerges clearly in the gospels that Jesus is not a man who makes himself God, but God who "makes himself" man (John 1:14).

When Jesus says, "Father," a vocative, it is not a blasphemy; rather, it is God talking to God, the Son speaking to the Father at the very heart of the inexpressible mystery of the Trinity. This is a profound intimacy—the intimacy of God with God, an intimacy beyond all intimacy, which exists nowhere but in the three-personed God, an intimacy besides which any other intimacy is a shadow, even our human intimacy with God, however great it might be.

The miracle of Gethsemane is that as witnesses of Christ's prayer, we are witnesses of this profound intimacy; in fact, we are witnesses every bit as much as the disciples, perhaps more so in that they were all asleep! I think we can say that their sleep corresponds to the fact that no one could really be a witness to the intimacy of the Son with the Father. If we are privileged in this way thanks to the accounts given us in the gospels, it is, once again, because the Holy Spirit makes us witnesses. He gives us this grace of being witnesses, but rather special ones, witnesses who didn't see anything. We are witnesses who saw nothing since none of us were there at Gethsemane. If we are witnesses, we are so only by the look of faith granted us by God.

## The Inexpressible

Mark, I believe, made a special effort to bring out the intimacy between the Father and the Son in the way he uses the word "Father." In fact, he is the only one of the four evangelists not to put the expression "my Father" in Jesus' mouth, although he does also say "your Father," speaking to them of God (11:25–26), or again, "the Father," in a more neutral manner (13:32). At no point in Mark does Jesus say "my Father," whereas in Luke he says this four times, in Matthew seventeen times, and in John twenty-six times! Never, anywhere in Mark do we hear Jesus say to God the vocative, "Father," except for here in Gethsemane, and this gives this prayer an exceptional forcefulness.

Mark proceeds in this way, I believe, to preserve the sanctity of the word "Father" as applied to God. It is similar to the way the Name of God was kept holy in Judaism. Another reason, it seems to me, is to capture the great reserve of Jesus, who doesn't speak in this way of God before others, not even his disciples. If we know that he said, "Father," in Gethsemane, we also know that he spoke like this only when his disciples were sleeping!

Mark seems to adopt the opposite attitude to Matthew, but the final result is the same. According to Matthew, nobody should be termed "Father" because God alone is our Father (23:9). In Mark, since so many men are called "father," the fatherhood of God, which transcends all other fatherhood, becomes difficult to convey. In Mark, Jesus exemplifies this because he doesn't, properly speaking, even say "my father," but, only ever says, "Abba." In short, Matthew and Mark both underline in their own way the immense gap between human paternity and the paternity of God.

If Mark proceeds as he does, it is without doubt because our bond with God, our Father, is not of the same order as the bond of Jesus with his Father. Our bond is the bond of adoption from the moment we become sons or children of God, while Jesus never did *become* a Son, having been so from all eternity. When we say that God is our Father, it has its basis in our systems of thought, and is therefore expressible; but when Jesus says that God is his Father, this is way beyond anything we can think and is really beyond expression. It is this inexpressibility which Mark conveys by not putting "my Father" into Jesus' mouth.

The moment *par excellence* that gave Jesus the opportunity to say to God, "my Father," was undoubtedly his baptism. On that day he is told by "a voice" (another way of designating the Father without naming him), "You are my beloved Son, on whom rests all my affection" (1:11). A statement like this would expect to generate a response, but Jesus is simply silent. This is the silence of an extreme reserve which keeps the expected response hidden in the heart.

## "Abba"

Mark was correct; the word "Father" does not have the same resonance, the same intensity of love, the same depth of tenderness on the lips of the Son as on ours . . . the distance between the two is beyond measure, unfathomable. It is the distance between the love within the trinity and our own love for God. Mark no doubt wished to refer to this gulf, in distinction from the other evangelists, by carefully transmitting to us the exact word used by Jesus in his Gethsemane prayer, "Abba."

"Abba": the word is not from the Hebrew, the holy, solemn, liturgical language of Jesus' time, but from Aramean which was the popular language, more familiar and doubtless more intimate, but still a million miles from the real intimacy between Father and Son.

"Abba": Mark also feels obliged to translate the word, giving its Greek equivalent, *pater*, "Father," but knowing all along the gulf that remains unfathomable between this translation and what lies in Jesus' heart when he addresses his Father as "Abba!"

"Abba": an ineffable word that we cannot begin to understand except on our knees, which is where Jesus himself spoke it that night in the garden on the mount of Olives (see Luke 22:41).

"Abba": in saying this, Jesus speaks of the inexpressible bond of humble love that unites him with the Father; he doesn't speak it before us, his disciples, but only before his Father, and it is the Spirit alone who enables us to be witnesses.

"Abba": Jesus speaks the inexpressible, and he speaks it "on his knees," in the extreme humility of his humanity, although he is God. How humble God is, more humble than men.

"Abba": Jesus gives voice to what is beyond words, in the inexpressible intimacy of the one who from all eternity was "in the bosom of the Father" (John 1:18).

"Abba": this is his prayer on the bosom of his Father.

"Abba": The Son says this to the Father from all eternity and to all eternity, from the beginning without beginning, when the Son was the

Son and the Father was the Father; the vocative attests that from all eternity God is both Father and Son in the mystery of the Holy Spirit.

"Abba": Christ, at one and the same time visibly man and invisibly God, makes this prayer both before our eyes, his face to the ground, as Matthew thinks (26:39), and invisibly on the bosom of the Father.

## When You Pray say "Father"

"Abba," Jesus said in the garden, at a distance from the disciples, not out of any desire to keep them in the dark about this way of praying, but because of his natural reserve. In fact, when Jesus teaches prayer, he provides them with the appropriate way to address God, inviting them to call him "Father" (Luke 11:2). This is not inciting them to blasphemy, but rather opening the door to the Father's heart, giving them an entrance into the mystery of intimacy to the degree it is given to each to perceive. This is truly a gift that Christ gives us.

It is this mysterious and sublime gift which Paul the apostle celebrates when he tells us that the Holy Spirit enables us to say "Abba" to the Father in our prayer (Rom 8:15; Gal 4:6). In fact, the gift is to say this alongside Christ, who has opened the door to the Father's heart for us; to say it with him, or more exactly and mysteriously "in him," in the bosom of the Father; the gift is to say it with immense gratitude since the gift surpasses all measure and all understanding—in the bosom of the Father, in Christ!

It is only in Christ that we can say "Abba, Father" because he alone can lead us to the Father in the power of the Holy Spirit. To say "Father" without being in Christ would be to commit blasphemy; to say it in him is an inestimable gift because to pray like this is to "become" children of God (John 1:12). It is to become what he is from all eternity, to become "partakers of the divine nature" (2 Pet 1:4), participants in the mystery of the Trinity in a way that escapes the understanding but which we can welcome and celebrate as an immeasurable and inexpressible grace. With this one word, prayer can immerse us in silence, a silence which is profound communion with the silence of God.

"When you pray, say, Father." What a wonder this is, the wonder of being able to say "Father" without blaspheming. To be able to say "Father" in the secrecy of a love given us to share by Christ, given us by the Father who awaits us in silence, just as he did in the garden of Olivet, a garden which comes to resemble the garden of Eden. The silence of the Father, deeply moved as he welcomes his children onto his breast. It is the silence of tenderness which welcomes our prayer, and is not offended if uttering this one word moves us too much to be able to say any more. It is a silence which welcomes our silence into the deep places of tenderness; a silence in which his and ours become one with that of the Holy Spirit and that of the Son as he rests on the bosom of the Father.

Reader friend, there are moments when we come to understand that the Son is welcoming us in silence with him into the bosom, onto the breast of the Father.

This is humble love, full of tenderness.

If no one before Jesus had ever called God his Father, though this was something God had longed for, no doubt it's because no one had previously been able to grasp this reality and take their place as a son or daughter of God. How indeed is one to be his son? How is one to live in this relation with God, even if only to our humble measure? Who will teach us to be a daughter? This is what Jesus is, and what he offers to us. To follow Christ and to be his disciple is to learn to become a son in his school. To be a daughter is to have learned to say, "Your will be done and not mine," in humble obedience and renunciation of our own will.

We will begin by considering our Master and listening to his prayer, before following him.

## "Take this cup from me"

The cup that Jesus is speaking of is a very particular cup, which he goes on to identify—it is exactly "this" cup.

"This cup" is an expression which means that it is right there before him, not being handed to him by men or even by the devil, but by God himself, which is who he asks to remove it. It is the Father who is holding this cup out to the Son, as Jesus himself will clearly state to Peter: "Shall I not drink the cup which the Father has given me to drink?" (John 18:11).

This cup is easy to identify since throughout the Bible there is only one cup to be found in God's hand. In the Old Testament, another cup exists and should be considered, "the cup of salvation" (Ps 116:13); however, this cup is in the hand of man, who raises it towards God, not in God's hand being offered to man. The only cup which God offers is the subject of a lengthy oracle in Jeremiah (25:15–38), to which we might add an allusion in one verse from a psalm (75:9).

Jeremiah's oracle teaches us that the cup contains "the wine of the wrath of God," which is to say the anger triggered in God by men's sins, not only those of his particular people, but those of all nations—the sins of the world. The result of the sins of all the nations is this cup, the contents of which Jeremiah is required by God to give to all the nations to drink. Its contents are extremely bitter, and cause all those who drink it to stagger. All the nations drank it at Jeremiah's word; this is made clear by the series of catastrophes of the period, and in Israel's case in particular, by the fall of Jerusalem, the destruction of the temple, and the deportation of the king and the people. This cup of the wine of God's wrath was bitter, extremely bitter.

Since Jeremiah's time, this cup had filled up again because men had not ceased to sin, and it seemed the disasters had served no purpose. Nothing had changed in the relationship between God and man. The cup was full again, but who was to drink it this time? How could it come to really mean something, to bring with it a change in men's hearts?

In Gethsemane we discover something entirely new, unexpected perhaps, and certainly unprecedented. The cup is not being offered by God to men, but by God to . . . God! God himself would drink the cup given by the Father to the Son, in the mystery of a secret divine decision within the Trinity. The decision may escape our understanding, but we can measure one extraordinary consequence of it: it will not be people whom God will cause to drink from the cup of his wrath. There couldn't be any better news! But what about the Son? Here in the garden our eyes rest on him and we ask ourselves in silence, "Will he drink it? Will he drink it alone? Will he drain it to the last drop?" If we manage to catch just a glimpse of what the anger caused to God by the world might represent in terms of immeasurable suffering for the Son, then we will understand his plea, on his knees, prostrate, face to the ground—"Father if it is possible, take this cup away from me!"

To drink the cup to the last drop is the way of Christ's Passion, a way of extreme pain, to the point of death.

On his knees, the Son pleads with the Father, but does not rebel. Rebellion does not take place on one's knees, face to the ground! A rebel stands, perhaps with his fist raised. Christ does not rebel but pleads; if there is any rebellion, it is ours when we see this cup being proffered by a father to his son.

Before following Jesus' way to the cross any further, I want to say something to defuse any mutinous feelings, or just as reassurance. We know that the Son accepts the cup and drinks it all; this is extraordinary, but the accounts describing the way of the cross reveal something else equally out of the ordinary, but which is more hidden. They reveal a Father who is totally invisible, but who is shown as very close to his Son, in a proximity which is marvelously compassionate; he is a Father who accompanies his Son to the very end, experiencing his death alongside him, with a love so great that the Son can draw from his Father the strength needed to drink the whole cup. Such is the bottomless mystery of the communion of love between Father and Son.

The purpose of what we have just said is to chase from our hearts any suggestion that would lead to a cry of injustice or of sadism, and sink into blasphemy. We don't want to allow what we see described in the narrative—that is, Christ, in his visible humanity moving towards the cross—to incite any rebellion or even blasphemy. We must also discern what is invisible in the text and escapes our eyes—the Father astonishingly closely tied to his Son by an inexpressible love. This is so very important if we are to properly receive the depth of the gospel accounts. We will be able to discover in this way that, alongside the Son who takes everything upon himself, we also find the Father who, in a hidden way, also takes it all on himself.

## "Father, if it is possible"

"Father, if it is possible . . ." says Christ. It certainly is possible; all things are possible to God, including the removal of this cup. Jesus knows this very well, as he also knows that he could refuse to drink it, and at this last moment push it away, in the great liberty his Father grants him. The Son knows this very well, having received from his Father all power and all authority (John 13:3), including that of saying "no" to his Father. Drinking the cup is in no way an imposition of the Father on the Son, as would be the case with an authoritarian father with no respect for his son's freedom.

Jesus knows all this, which is why the Father has no need to reply. The Father doesn't respond because the Son knows what the reply would be. In fact, he has even provided it himself, John tells us, in a very similar situation: "Now my soul is troubled; but what shall I say? Father, deliver me from this hour? But it is for this very thing that I came" (John 12:27).

Christ knows that the decision to go to the cross is their shared decision, their common project to rescue the whole of humanity. Jesus knows that the will of the Father and the Son are one, sealed by the Holy Spirit.

Jesus had already denied the possibility of the query, "Father, if it is possible . . ." On each occasion he had told his disciples, "It is necessary that I die." Jesus' own response to this "is it possible?" is "No, it is necessary!" This "it is necessary" of the Passion is never spoken by the Father, but always and only by the Son.

What is the meaning of the "it is necessary" which Jesus freely adopts throughout his ministry? Would it be akin to a fate which cannot be avoided? Not at all. We should recall, reader friend, that the word "fate" (*eimarmenē*) or "destiny" is alien to the biblical lexicon and even to biblical thought. Fate is a Greek concept from Greek philosophy, which presents fate as a law above all others, superior even to the gods. Nobody, not even Zeus himself, could escape destiny or fate.

In the Bible there is no law governing God. God is sovereignly free, the Father as much as the Son or the Holy Spirit. The "it is necessary" expresses a logic which is not that of anger or vengeance, but of love, a logic dictated by God himself and drawn from the bottomless depths of his love.

It is in the logic of divine love that each divine decision is reached and brought to its fulfilment by God himself. It is in this love, in this logic of love, that the way of Christ's cross opens up and is adopted for the salvation of humanity, a logic settled on from all eternity when God takes it upon himself to drink the cup. The Father gives the cup to the Son, which he receives freely, in love. The Son receives all the necessary strength to reach the goal of this logic, of this project, of this shared decision—and this also includes the prospect of the resurrection. We must not forget that each time Christ says "it is necessary" that he die, he doesn't leave it there but continues so that this first "it is necessary" becomes "it is necessary" that he be raised (by the Father).

The logic of divine love is the logic of love, which transforms death in the resurrection.

The Father and the Son are to engage the logic of the way of the cross together, each in his own way, but in an inseparable communion of love.

## "Your will be done"

When Jesus gets to Gethsemane, something within him has changed; his horizon is suddenly reduced, darkened, restricted. Where not long before, en route to Gethsemane, he had still been able to speak to the disciples of his resurrection, his horizon now is not so high; it stops at dying. "My soul is sorrowful even unto death," he tells them as they enter the garden (Matt 26:38; Mark 14:34). His outlook does not reach beyond death. Then he "began to be distressed and anguished," as Mark notes (14:33), and even to think about drawing back. The task before him suddenly seems too much for his strength. How will he manage to take the cup? From where will he draw the strength he needs to drink it to the end, which is to say, to the point of death? Jesus is reckoning up his human strength, and finding it to be limited. Where is he to gather the strength to hope when his perspective does not go beyond the death which is approaching? Who will give him the strength he needs, and of which, in his anguish and humanity, he feels destitute? Distress and anguish have a more or less paralyzing effect on people, including Jesus, who in his humanity finds himself confronted by just that reality. "Love is strong as death" (Song 8:6), one remembers, but not "stronger" than death! Jesus knows himself to be God, but at this moment the human reality is pulling him down, down beneath the weight of pain. Does the summons of the cup contain in itself a hint of hope from which to draw strength? Not at all, on the contrary even: it is a truly terrible summons; it has no horizon other than death. There still remain the disciples who are there, and Jesus now invites them to pray with him (Matt 26:38). There is something comforting in this "with him," but it is also rather poignant, since Jesus knows how weak they are. He must have known that for no reason at all they would soon be asleep; after all, they were only men! There was no strength in them to help him to grasp the cup and drink. Unable to count on his own frail humanity, or on his disciples, there remained only his Father, so it is to him that he turns, first of all to tell him very humbly about the human weakness which is pulling him down; "Father, if it is possible, take this cup away from me!" Then Jesus feels impelled to go further. He had so often preached faith to others, "take no anxious thought for the morrow . . ." He knows that he cannot trust his own limited human strength, as he confirms, but he can trust God and the reinforcement God will give right on time and not before. Now he needs to have faith, to expect, to have absolute confidence in his Father, without yet having received from him the strength to fulfill his will; this would be an act of complete faith. The will of God is always beyond our human ability alone, and this is so as to require of us faith. Jesus' expectation is that God will provide the strength, but first he needs to say "yes," the yes of total faith; not only the yes he has always said to the Father in the reality of his deity, but the yes of his human frailty, the submission of his human will which pulls him to draw back and quit; he must submit his will to the will of the Father. He knows very well what the Father's will is because it is why he came to the earth (John 5:30, 6:38 . . . ), but he needs now to submit his human will to the divine will. It is in an act of complete faith that Jesus then says, "Father, may your will be done, not mine."

Gethsemane has often been presented as a moment in which a division, or opposition appears between the Father and the Son in the heart of the Trinity. However, I believe the church Fathers were quite right to reject this view; if there were a division between the Father and the Son it would be a victory for the Adversary right at the heart of the Trinity. This is wrong, as we will confirm along the way to Christ's cross. The conflict which we glimpse here is within Christ himself, between his human will and his divine will. The Adversary is at work and is endeavoring to gain a foothold in Jesus' heart, and cause him to flounder. Jesus, however, reasserts himself and resists, even before he prays. His perspective may be clouded and may prevent him from seeing clearly, but it cannot impede the exercise of his faith. Christ does not draw back; the temptation to recoil in anguish when faced with the cup passes in a moment, lasting no more than an instant, and he re-gathers himself and stretches out his hand in faith to take it. The Adversary attacked the human weakness in order to shake Christ, but in vain. He comes up against the confidence which unites the Son with his Father. Christ has not allowed his humanity to take the upper hand over his divinity, but humbly commits his humanity to God.

The Father listens to the prayer of the Son in silence. He does not intervene, not that he wants to leave him alone to suffer, but out of respect for his human freedom, the freedom to pull back and decline to drink the cup. The Father fully respects human liberty, and places confidence in it. He has confidence in this Galilean who has always trusted him. He fully trusts and hopes; the immense trust, full of hope, which God has placed in man and which has always been disappointed, is now focused on Christ, the perfect man. God's deep silence is full of hope in this man from Nazareth, a magnificent and overwhelming silence. The situation is very fragile, with all the fragility of humanity, which could compromise the whole divine project—so fragile! The fate of humanity hangs on this fragility, hangs on the "yes" so earnestly awaited by God, a "yes" which must be given freely by this man who lacks even the support of his sleeping brothers.

O Christ, we were all asleep while you were on your knees and carried on your shoulders alone the fate of humanity. We slept while the life of the world was at risk. We slept, and you could no longer count on anything from us. We slept while you said yes . . . humbly, on your knees, out of love for us.

O Christ, may you be forever praised!

## The Father's Response to the Son

To our eyes, as reported by Matthew and Mark, God doesn't seem to respond to the prayer of his Son, doesn't react. There is something in this which is very shocking to us. The only thing we sense from God is his silence, and this seems to be the silence of absence or indifference. We are also aware of the distress and anguish of Jesus (Mark 14:33), his profound unrest in the face of death. But there is another factor we are allowed to see, as recorded by John, who describes Christ leaving Gethsemane at the moment of his arrest. This is a Christ who is no longer anguished, but, on the contrary, is filled with such power that the men who come to take him fall backwards to the ground (18:6). Obviously something happened between his arriving in Gethsemane and leaving, something humanly inexplicable. In short, we have a silent Father, playing no part, and a Son who is transformed, revived in a more than human, extraordinary way. So much is this so that we see an ordinary man causing others to fall over backwards simply by opening his mouth and saying, "I am he." Something happened, but what exactly?

Everything is made clear in Luke, and in an amazing way, because what we are told was in fact hidden from any witness except for Christ; it could only have been revealed to Luke by the Holy Spirit; he alone can search the depths of God and reveal to us what took place at the heart of the Trinity, between the Father and the Son.

We will listen to what Luke says, received from the Holy Spirit; but we must not forget, reader friend, that there are many times when to our eyes, God says and does nothing, fails to intervene and seems distant and absent, when in fact, albeit in a discreet, humble way that is hidden from our eyes, he is indeed there, engaging magnificently in his imperceptible and humble love.

> [39]Jesus went, as was his custom, to the mount of Olives and his disciples followed him. [40]When he arrived there, he said to them, "Pray that you enter not into temptation." [41]Then he

withdrew from them about the distance of a stone's throw, knelt down and prayed, saying, [42]"If it be your will, take away from me this cup! Nevertheless, not my will be done, but yours." [43]Then an angel appeared to him from heaven, strengthening him. [44]Being in great distress, he prayed more earnestly, and his sweat became as drops of blood which fell to the ground. [45]After he had prayed he stood and went to the disciples who he found asleep with heaviness; [46]"Why are you sleeping," he said, "awake and pray that you enter not into temptation." (Luke 22:39–46)

## "An angel appeared to him from heaven, strengthening him"

The Father's answer to the prayer is given to the Son immediately, without the slightest delay, without him so much as waiting until the end of the prayer; it is given while the Son is still praying, with an extraordinary immediacy, perhaps beyond even what Christ might have expected. That is certainly in the text if we look closely; Luke tells us that Christ began to pray as he knelt down (v. 41), and that he stood up "after praying" to rejoin the disciples (v. 45). Between these actions, that is, while he was praying, the Father's answer is evident in the appearance of an angel (v. 43).

The angel who comes from heaven is therefore an angel from God, which is to say from the Father. This angel who "appears" makes apparent the invisible presence of the Father; his presence puts an end to any doubts on the subject—the Father is manifestly there through the person of the angel, communicating his presence unambiguously to his Son.

Between the angel and God there is a very particular connection, one that is stronger than we may think. This is seen specifically in the account of the burning bush (Exod 3). This account tells us that "an angel appeared" (3:2), the same expression as here, in the midst of a bush; but then, immediately afterwards, the voice that spoke from the bush was that not of the angel but of God (3:4). Moses understood that, through the angel, God himself was present, which was why he covered his face—not for fear at seeing the angel, but for fear of God (3:6). Moses was not mistaken, as God confirmed to him when he immediately showed Moses that it was indeed he, God, who was showing himself by means of the angel (3:16). The angel did not meanwhile disappear; he was not sidelined but was really there, and yet less so than God, who was very present, invisibly, by means of the visible angel. That the invisible God was more present than the visible angel is very apparent in this story of the burning bush.

It is just as clear in Jesus' case as it was for Moses; an angel appears to him, but in reality it is the Father who is there by means of the angel, and more present than the angel.

The angel "strengthens" Christ, Luke tells us, which is to say that through the angel, the Father is marvelously strengthening the Son. At the moment of the Son's extreme weakness, the appearance of the angel brings the strength of the Father's presence. It is enough for Christ to see the angel, and everything changes; he receives amazing strength from the revelation of the one he loves.

We see, then, that through the angel the Father is there, demonstrating his presence to his Son. He does this during the time of prayer, before he has even finished praying, in an extraordinary response to the Son.

Jesus had not asked or claimed the presence of this angel, but nevertheless, there he is: a sign of pure grace from the Father. The Father knows how to give exactly what is needed, even to those who haven't asked.

## A Silent Angel

An angel by definition is a messenger, one who carries a message. This is their primary function, the reason for their presence and arrival. An angel appeared to Zacharias as the carrier of a message (Luke 1:13); the same with Mary (1:31), with the shepherds near Bethlehem (2:11), and with so many others in the Old Testament too. But here we have an angel who doesn't bring any word—he says nothing. He is a strange and extraordinary messenger; his message, in fact, is beyond words, in the unspoken realm of silence; his message is the silence of the Father's compassion for his agonized Son, and flows from the Father's tenderness, in that love beyond all other loves for which there are no words. The angel here is overflowing with the inexpressible, with the silent love of the Father for his Son, and this silence has an amazing power, which indeed is what so strengthens Christ. He has no need to hear the angel speak; it is enough just to see him and look at him since his mere appearance says more than any words. The angel bespeaks the silence of God in which there is nothing distant, heavy, or empty, and he conveys its extraordinary beneficence; it is a silence full of the Father. What an upending this is of our understanding of God's silence!

"An angel appeared to him." The angel appeared to Jesus alone, and not to the disciples. It is true that the disciples were sleeping, but, as we know, angels do appear to people in their sleep, as for example with Joseph (Matt 1:20, 2:13). The angel could also have awoken the disciples, but he is not there for them or for some kind of display; he is just humbly there for the Son alone. The Father is humble, unseen, and unnoticed by anyone, appearing to the Son alone; he is silent, awaking no one, coming to enjoy a depth of intimacy with the Son at the heart of the mystery of the trinity, in wonderful humility.

Luke was not one of the twelve, was not present at Gethsemane, and none of the twelve could have told him about the angelic appearance since Jesus himself said nothing when he went to wake them. Jesus, as humbly as his Father, made no great deal out of the angel's appearance; like Father, like Son! Luke could only have received this information from the Holy Spirit, the sole witness of the intimacy between Father and Son. He received the information in a very sober form of words, in the most modest way possible, not for the benefit of our curiosity, but for our edification.

## The Strength Received

The angel came to strengthen Jesus, and the Greek word (*en-iskuō*) tells us that the strengthening was interior. It was strength received from the outside—from heaven, from the Father—and it came into the Son to merge with his strength which was so shaky. It worked by synergy, multiplying his strength many times over, increasing it without measure, because synergy with God is indeed beyond all measure.

It was a power that came to compensate for the failing, in fact non-existent, strength of the disciples. To see them sleeping would be discouraging, but to see an angel of God could only encourage to the highest degree.

At the river Jordan, the Father had spoken his love to the Son, as well as on the mount of Transfiguration; but here, nothing! The Father may not have spoken his love, but he does demonstrate it very concretely; it goes well beyond words in a way that is so functional and humble. There is no "heaven opening" (Luke 3:21), no "luminous cloud" (Matt 17:5), no "Holy Spirit descending in the form of a dove," just a simple angel in the night, appearing without any brilliance, an angel who discreetly implants new strength deep in Jesus' heart.

It is this power that the soldiers experience to their cost when they come to arrest Jesus, not knowing where it comes from; however, we do know, thanks to the Holy Spirit, who revealed it to Luke.

Why was the power necessary? Surely not just to deal with the soldiers! It was to give Christ the strength to be able to grasp the cup and to drink it to the dregs; which is to say, the strength to accept the failure, denial, and defection of the disciples, to bear up under the false witnesses, the blows, the humiliation of slaps and spitting, the whipping and the insults; the strength to face finding himself alone and to die submitted to the mockery of the soldiers; the strength to bear the sins of the world, to continue to love, to hope, to trust, to persevere; the strength to follow step by step the way of the cross . . . superhuman strength received from the Father and from him alone, by means of this angel among the olive trees of Gethsemane. In this way, we see how the Father is there, unfailingly, to give to the Son all that he needs; it is the silent strength of a silent Father, who is wonderfully present beyond anything we could think; an unfailing strength which conveys in silence the immeasurable depths of the communion of tenderness and love between the Father and the Son.

How wonderful you are, Father, to be so marvelously present in your silence!

The angel does not appear *before* the prayer, not as an enabler giving Christ strength to say yes to the cross. The yes had to be spoken by the Son alone, not by the Son with added strength from the Father. As soon as the word is pronounced by the Son in all his human weakness, immediately the Father, without delay, gives him the strength to give the word action, to move from acceptance to accomplishment, from the desire to obey to obedience itself. How wonderful it is for us too to know this, that God loves us enough to give us the strength to accomplish whatever task corresponds to his will for us, and which we wish to accomplish out of obedience to him.

How wonderful you are, Father, to be so marvelously present in your silence to us too!

Reader friend, our part is first of all to freely say yes to God, and then to trust him to help us bring it to pass.

# The Battle

After describing the appearance of the angel, Luke continues his account with another detail not found in the other gospels. He tells us that Jesus is in a battle, a struggle, strife (struggle is the primary sense of the word *agonia* from which our word agony comes; see v. 44). This struggle is of no common intensity, as we see when we consider the detail Luke provides us next: "his sweat became as drops of blood which fell to the ground"; it is a struggle with an impressive physical dimension.

Here, then, is Jesus in intense combat, but with another feature which is very surprising to us: the adversary with whom he is fighting is not named. Luke doesn't say anything in his account right here, but his gospel is constructed in such a way that he has already told us what to understand.

Could it be that Jesus was struggling with the angel or that the angel had provoked him? Well, of course not; we know that on the contrary, the angel came to strengthen him, and strengthening is the role of an ally, not an adversary. If the angel is an ally, God is equally so, having sent his Son the support of his messenger. I feel obliged to make this point very clear because I have read commentaries on this text which present Jesus as struggling with God, a little like Jacob at the ford over the Jabbok (Gen 32:24). There is nothing of this at Gethsemane, it seems to me; the angel sent by the Father to help the Son shows that the Father is standing alongside his Son, to sustain him in the battle as a powerful ally.

Who then is the anonymous adversary? I have said Luke constructed his gospel so that this can be understood; it is a precise point, and concerns another detail stated only by Luke in his account of Jesus' temptation in the wilderness. Luke concludes his account with a statement added by neither Matthew nor Mark: "after the devil had finished tempting him, he left him until a more favorable occasion" (4:13). This is a piece of information which should awaken the reader's interest to look for the "favorable occasion" when the devil would choose to tempt Jesus again. It is right here that the favorable occasion has arisen, here in Gethsemane, in the darkness of this Passion night.

This, then, is the enemy who comes to attack Jesus. He is unnamed by Luke, thus demonstrating the way the adversary hides himself, how he prowled in the darkness of Olivet. He so cloaks himself that Jesus calls him "the power of darkness," as Luke indeed tells us (22:53). It is with this redoubtable power that Jesus must now struggle.

Satan had already attacked Judas, as Luke again informs us with the terrible expression, "Satan entered into Judas" (22:3). Satan, then, had found enough darkness in the heart of this disciple to take up residence. There was no darkness in Jesus, but the darkness around him was thick, and Satan approaches to do combat with the Master, having overcome the disciple.

Not only had Judas been overcome, but Satan had also fastened his desire on the other disciples, just as Jesus had informed Peter just a few hours before Gethsemane; "Simon! Simon! Satan has desired to sift you, as wheat is sifted . . ." (22:31).

The disciples were therefore also engaged in a battle, and this caused Jesus to give them this salutary instruction the moment they reached Gethsemane, "Pray, so that you enter not into temptation" (22:40). Saying this to the disciples when they got to Gethsemane shows the degree to which Jesus was aware and vigilant, feeling the lurking presence of the Adversary, who, however, sought to assail him rather than them. Indeed the close of the wilderness temptation story makes clear that Satan's sights were set not on the disciples but on Jesus himself, and so it is in Gethsemane that we find this very violent struggle of Jesus against Satan, a struggle so fierce that "his sweat became drops of blood which fell to the ground."

## The Father's Help

This struggle was not the wish of the Father; it was not a sadistic Father who fomented the battle and pushed the Son towards the Tempter. God is not like that; but neither did he spare the Son from having to go through such a fight in order that Satan might finally and decisively be vanquished by a man. This could surely be by none other than Christ, who alone had his measure. The Father, however, is not passive; in anticipation of the struggle he gives the Son the necessary strength to confront the Adversary, which is why, just beforehand, he sends the angel to "strengthen" him. The first purpose of this influx of strength from the Father through the angel is to combat Satan. The Father therefore is his Son's main helper in the struggle, full of prescience on his behalf. David celebrated the Lord, saying, with the same verb *enischuō*, "You strengthen me for war" (2 Sam 22:40). Christ could appropriate the same verse and also say, as he prays in Gethsemane, "Father, you strengthen me for the struggle."

When Satan attacks Christ, Christ has just said yes to his Father, and yes to fulfilling his will. The Son, in both his humanity and his deity, is now in perfect communion with the Father, with one single will and desire. The Son, "on his knees," is prostrated before God in an attitude which passes from supplication to adoration. At the bottom of his heart, he has the strength from the angel to carry him to the full accomplishment of the divine plan.

The profound union of the Father and the Son is what faces Satan. Lest we be mistaken about this, what Satan wants is not the death of humanity but that humanity bow before him rather than God; this included Jesus, as he had said to him in the wilderness, "If you will bow before me . . ." (4:7). The Devil—in Greek *diabolos*, the Divider—wishes to divide any communion between humanity and God every bit as he much as he detests the union of the Father and the Son. In Gethsemane, as in the wilderness, the Jealous One wants the Son to prostrate himself before him and not before God, wishing in some sort to take the place of the Father; what supreme pride in the Adversary!

## The Power of Humility

In the face of this assault, Christ needs to do more than persevere in prayer; he needs to "pray more intensely," as Luke says (v. 44), with an intensity of prayer equal to the intensity of the battle, which is to say, for us, beyond measure. We have none of us ever sweat blood in prayer, as none of us have ever been engaged in such a battle. The Adversary takes hold against the very unity of the Trinity. It took unimagined pride to grasp at the Son's union with the Father in the Holy Spirit. Christ resists to the point of sweating blood, not in his own strength but in the synergy of trinitarian strength deposited in him by the angel. What is this strength or power which is superior to pride? It is divine humility, which is Satan's constant stumbling-block. The humble love of God alone is victorious over Satan. The divine unity provokes the Divider, but the unity of humble, divine love is unceasingly victorious. The appearance of the angel who strengthens Christ fully manifests this humble love.

Human humility is an astonishing force, the reality of which many of us don't suspect; divine humility is an infinitely greater force, the extent of which, Satan, swollen with pride, fails to perceive and against which he can do nothing.

## The Silent Struggle

As astonishing as it may seem, the struggle in Gethsemane was completely silent. Neither Jesus nor Satan said a word, unlike the temptations in the wilderness which consisted entirely of dialogue, or Adam's temptation in the Garden of Eden (Gen 3). In the wilderness, Jesus refuted the temptations of his adversary one by one, and it was for something similar that he prepared his disciples, telling them in Gethesemane, "Pray that you enter not into temptation," which is to say, don't starting talking to the Tempter; speak to God and not to the Enemy, so that you don't waste time in words with someone who is more adept at argument than you!

Jesus does much more than that here—more than all of us and more than the disciples. He takes a place above words and, rather than the temptations, confronts the Tempter himself, in a way none of us could. There would be no need to sweat blood in a struggle against words or ideas; if Jesus sweats blood as he did, it is because his whole being is engaged in combat with the very being of the Malign one, beyond words, in silence, in hand to hand combat so to speak, in a struggle in which very great strength was needed. The strength available to Jesus is that of the silent synergy of humble trinitarian love.

Luke says nothing more because it is beyond our understanding. That night, however, as they all slept, this great struggle was conducted against the power of darkness in an impressive depth of silence.

The result of the struggle is not actually stated; it is barely evoked, no more than suggested by Luke. It does not, however, escape us if we pay careful attention to Luke's choice of words. After being on his knees throughout his prayer, when Jesus stands up, he does so in the strength received from the angel. Now, when he says that Jesus "stood up" (which neither Matthew of Mark tell us), Luke uses a word that pertains to resurrection (*anistēmi*, cf. 18:33, 24:7). Elsewhere, in speaking of the disciples' sleep, Luke uses a different word to the one chosen by Matthew and Mark (*katheudō*). He speaks of their sleep with a verb which means "to be asleep" (*koimaō*) and clearly has a connotation of death; in fact it is the verb translated as "to die" in Matt 27:52, Acts 13:36. The two verbs, "to stand up" and "to be asleep," show that Jesus received power from the angel to rise from among the sleepers, which beyond doubt is a discreet allusion to Easter, to the power Jesus received from his Father to rise from among the dead. If this is truly so, then the strength Christ received on the mount of Olives is the strength which enabled him to go right through, to conquer sin and hell and to rise from the grave. It is an unprecedented strength, beyond anything we can imagine, strength which the Father alone could give. Indeed, it is given to him now, silently and humbly, in the midst of the garden and the sleeping disciples, at the moment the Son receives from him the cup to drink.

This Christ—on his feet, rising from combat—is a victorious Christ, victorious over Satan, a Christ invested with his paschal majesty. As a result, it is not surprising to see the soldiers fall backwards before such majesty when they come to arrest Christ as he leaves Gethsemane.

## "Pray that you enter not into temptation"

We could perhaps stop here at this point where it goes beyond my ability to say any more, but I would like to pause now to think about our own struggle, for which Jesus prepares us when he says to his disciples, "Pray, that you enter not into temptation." According to Luke, these are the only words Jesus addresses to the disciples; the literary construction of this passage is remarkable, setting Jesus' struggle at the center of the two extremities where he issues the same invitation: "Pray, that you enter not into temptation" (vv. 40 and 46). Presented this way, Jesus' struggle in prayer is seen as the source of light which shines on us, illuminating our prayer in our struggles; using other terms, we could say that our prayer is peripheral to Christ's.

It is amazing to note that in our struggle against temptation, Jesus gives us no more than one weapon alone: prayer. There is nothing else, but this is enough.

Nevertheless, we should not forget what the Lord had said to Peter a little earlier, speaking of the Tempter: "Simon! Simon! Satan has desired to sift you as wheat; but I have prayed for you . . ." (Luke 22:32).

This is an extraordinary statement, which serves to keep us from any pride in our fight against the Adversary. Every victory against him does not in fact issue from *our* prayer, but from that of Christ, who prays for us in our struggles, prayer which is much more important than ours. Christ humbly does not repeat in Gethsemane that he is praying for his disciples; but we should not forget that he is doing so when we exert ourselves in prayer, praying for us even as he tells us, "Pray, that you enter not into temptation."

> O Christ, you who intercede for us without ceasing at the
> right hand of the Father,
> may you be praised for your prayer, which tirelessly bears us up
> in our struggles with temptation.
> Help us, by the grace of the Holy Spirit,
> that our prayers may always be in harmony with yours.

## The Weapon of Prayer

As astonishing as it may seem, Jesus didn't give his disciples any teaching about temptation, and gave them no counsel other than to pray. To know more about this subject, important as it is, our only recourse is to pray as he requires of us, and it is in prayer that we will be given what we need to resist the assaults of the Adversary.

Prayer, of course, but how? First of all, like Christ, humbly, on our knees before the Father. Humbly, in abandonment of will to the Father; humbly, not counting on any strength other than that given us by the Father; in silence, just as strength was given Christ in his prayer, whether with or without the appearance of an angel. What matters is the strength given to those who humbly recognize their unceasing need of this help to fight at the time of trial. God gives this help to humble people, mysteriously, as if in secret, silently, as if hiding himself, humble as he is. Humility in prayer is our only weapon, a weapon whose strength lies in its synergy with the immeasurable strength of God's humility. To cease prayer before or during combat is to cut ourselves off from this synergy, to sever ourselves from the source which gives us the strength necessary to meet each struggle. To pray is, in reality, to allow God to fight for us through our prayer.

Remarkably, Satan comes to fight us at the very heart of prayer. He insinuates himself with a multitude of thoughts which distract, frustrate and disperse our prayer. What should we then do against this adversary who slips into our prayer and endeavors to shatter it? Quite simply, what Jesus did! He too was praying when the adversary came to oppose him; the whole struggle unfolded during prayer. During prayer, his sweat dropped as blood, and it is not until afterwards that Luke tells us that Jesus arose from prayer. Jesus only ceased from prayer when the struggle was terminated. He therefore confronted the Adversary entirely in prayer, and by then praying with ever more insistence, not in his own strength but with the strength he received from his Father through the angel's appearance. If the Tempter attacks us during our prayer, what we need to do is redouble the prayer, counting on the strength we then receive from God.

God gives strength for prayer as he also gives strength to fight. The strength he gives for prayer is the same strength he gives for battle, and it is the strength of humble, divine love, the strength which keeps us in communion with God. When we pray, we receive in our human humility the strength of divine humility.

## Standing to Pray

Jesus prayed on his knees, and redoubled his prayer. It is not until he had finished that Luke tells us, "Jesus rose from prayer" (v. 45). Jesus leaves prayer and holds himself erect in an attitude that shows him victorious, as a conqueror over the power of darkness. He "rose up," as Luke says, using the verb which, as we have seen, already prefigures his emergence from the tomb, upright, into the early morning light of resurrection day.

It is this upright, victorious Christ who comes to awaken his sleeping disciples and invite them, a second time, to pray against temptation, but adding this time to what he said at first (v. 40) a preliminary word, as surprising as it is wonderful: "*Rise up* and pray, that you enter not into temptation! You will always have to fight and you can do it by praying on your knees like me when I was buffeted while you were sleeping; but you can also fight standing, as I am now. Upright, because my victory is now become yours. I am making you the beneficiaries of my victory. Pray standing, like the conquerors I am causing you to be, with the strength of conquerors, the strength received from the Father, and which I am sharing with you!" How wonderful!

Indeed, for the Eastern believer, the attitude par excellence to adopt for prayer is to stand upright, especially on Sundays, as a witness and celebration of the paschal victory.

The disciples were asleep throughout the struggle with Satan; they had not been witnesses of the victory; furthermore, it is a victory which Luke is unable to describe because it is beyond our understanding. No more than the disciples could we ever tell it. We can only lean and depend upon it as a certainty of faith, and then celebrate it, our hearts full of paschal joy.

# CHAPTER 4

# Before the Sanhedrin

A T FIRST SIGHT THIS episode ought not to hold our attention because there seems to be nothing here which distinctly concerns the Father. Effectively, he maintains an absolute silence without intervening in any way, so there doesn't seem to be the least sign which would indicate his presence.

Nevertheless, we see that there is good reason to pause here when we realize that the men before whom Jesus stands to be judged are exactly the same as those, the chief priests, the scribes and the elders, who a few days earlier had been gathered around him listening to the extraordinary parable of the vineyard. With that in mind, we now find ourselves at the precise moment when the well-beloved son arrives in the vineyard and finds himself in the presence of the tenants. For us, as perhaps for them, the silence of God is suddenly illuminated by a shining light, and takes on a new significance: we know that at this moment the heart of the Father is full of these few words—"they will respect my Son." When Jesus is before the Sanhedrin, God in his silence is occupied with the thought, "they will respect my Son." It is the silence of very close attention: the fate of the Well-Beloved Son is about to be played out. If he is to be condemned to death, this will take place now. The fate of the Son hangs on the decision of the tenants. What will they decide? Will the parable, as stated by Jesus, be effectuated?

Not only does God's silence become clear to us, but also his non-intervention. In fact, the Father will hold himself back from intervening because he has entire confidence in the tenants, the members of the Sanhedrin: "they will respect my Son." This great confidence is reinforced by a no less great hope. God absolutely respects the liberty of those to whom he has entrusted the vineyard, those to whom he has sent and entrusted Christ. There would be no point in God intervening: "they will respect my Son." What will happen during the trial?

The Son of God is there, very God of very God, standing before men who have become his judges! Heaven is silent in stupefaction! What profound darkness there must be in the hearts of men not to see that it is God who is on trial!

The Son is there, strengthened by the love of the Father, standing before his judges. In perfect communion with the Father and in accordance with their joint decision, he is ready to give his life, knowing full well that he will have to do so, and knowing perfectly the darkness of the human heart. He is ready in the superabundance of his love for people; but this doesn't mean that, along with the Father, his love would not cause him to hope that they, despite their darkened hearts, these men might do better than condemn him to death.

> What insane love of God for men!
> Lord Jesus Christ, Son of God, have pity on us, sinners!
> Father of infinite mercy, have pity on us, sinners!

## The False Witnesses

First of all there is a series of witnesses, all of whom are revealed as false, each of them as false as the others; this would be a first blow to the hope and trust of the Father. None of these false witnesses respects the Son. They all lie, but as Mark notes, the false witnesses don't agree among themselves (14:56), which does leave some ground for hope. Their testimony will carry little weight when it comes to the sentence. If the false witnesses cancel each other out, it might still be possible to hear a true witness, one who could save the life of the condemned man, as the word of Reuben had been enough to save Joseph. It was necessary to keep listening in silence, hoping that a reliable witness would eventually tell the truth.

Then, while waiting for the one true witness, the Father's heart receives a grievous blow; suddenly in the courtyard of the high priest's palace, a cock crows, a first time and then a second . . . In the silence that follows, the Father's heart bleeds silently; there had been a true witness, there in the courtyard, warming himself beside a meager fire, but what he says is so sad to hear, it would have been better if nothing at all had been spoken. Jesus simply turned and looked toward the courtyard and said nothing (Luke 22:61). The Father and the Son are united in the same grief, together with the Holy Spirit, who is silent as well, like a wounded dove.

It is only the bitter tears of repentance that will be joined to those of God. The disciple has left the courtyard to shed his tears of repentance in the secret of the night. The silent tears of the grieved God are mingled with his . . . what a silence!

## The Interrogation

Then the chief priest—whose name Mark respectfully declines to tell us—troubled by the silence, takes matters into his own hands and breaks in upon Jesus' quiet. "Do you answer nothing? What is it that these people are saying against you?" (14:60). Mark continues his account with the following few words, the depths of which we will never understand, "he kept his peace and answered not a word"! If only the chief priest had known that in the silence, so troubling to him, tears were flowing and mingling, tears of wounded tenderness and repentance.

The chief priest continued his interrogation with a question that was decisive, certainly, but containing a trap to induce Jesus to blaspheme: "Are you the Christ, the Son of the Blessed?" (14:61). To answer this formidable question, which burns with animosity, Jesus emerges from his silence and pronounces words which burn with another fire, a fire which does not consume. They are the same words Moses had heard spoken from the burning bush. Jesus, burning with the same fire, responds without hesitation, without discomposure, peacefully, "I am."

The members of the Sanhedrin have no need of further discussion; they understand very well what Jesus wished to say. They now have a choice to make: either they cry blasphemy, or they take off their shoes as Moses had done and bow before the one who alone can say "I am who I am" (Exod 3:14), because he alone is God, very God of very God.

For God the Father, this is an essential moment, of immense importance; how would the vineyard tenants react. The reply given by his Son to the chief priest is so true, so beautiful, so clear that his Father heart vibrates with hope: "They will respect my Son; they cannot but respect him as he reveals himself to them, very God of very God, my Son, my only, my well-beloved!"

But the chief priest does not remove his shoes; instead, he rips his vestment as a sign of horror, and calls out to the others, "You have heard the blasphemy! What do you think?"

## The Verdict

The verdict has only been suggested and not yet pronounced; the chief priest awaits the approbation of the rest. It is a moment of unbelievable intensity. Here, indeed, the fate of the son is in the hands of the tenants. Between the chief priest's question and the response of the Sanhedrin's other members there is a lapse of time of incalculable length and extreme gravity. Christ is silent, awaiting the response which will determine his fate. The Father is silent too. Will there be one wise man among the leaders to propose an alternative to the chief priest? Will there be a Reuben among them? Will Nicodemus intervene? Anything is still possible. The Father and the Son are united in a common hope: they can still have confidence. They can feel this way all the more because in the Law of Israel there was a verse which opened the door to hope and trust, a door which the ancient rabbis had marvelously discovered and recorded in the Targum; it was a door that would have been well known to all these specialists in the Law gathered together in the Sanhedrin; a door which you are perhaps unfamiliar with, reader friend, but which, once revealed, will help you understand why God's hope in the rulers of the people could persist, and why he could still think, "They will respect my Son."

In the Law of Israel, there is an article which deals with blasphemy. It specifies that those who blaspheme the name of God should be condemned to death (Lev 24:10–16). It is a severe article, but closer examination, with the great kindness constantly evinced by God in mind, led the ancients, with God's help, to formulate a further article of great clemency. Praise God for inspiring this clemency in the ancients, from which Christ could now hope to benefit; hope was still possible. It just needed one person who knew the Tradition well and who also had this clemency in his heart, to now recall this tradition of the ancients to the others, and Christ would be spared.

The text recording this tradition is quite long because it deals with four different cases at once. The following is just the part that concerns blaspheming the holy Name.

> This is what Moses decided, with the agreement of the Highest. In the case of the man who blasphemed the holy Name, Moses said, "I heard nothing." He said this to teach the judges who were before him to proceed slowly in capital cases, in order not to have anyone who might be judged worthy of the death penalty put to death precipitately, lest it be found that there were further points in his defense; and also so that they

would not be ashamed to say, "we heard nothing," since Moses, their Master, had also said, "I heard nothing." (Targum Neophiti, Lev 24:12)[1]

This is a rather fine forbearance on the part of the tradition, which is even presented as having God's approval, "the agreement of the Highest." It sufficed therefore for the judges to say that they had not heard the blasphemy and the life of the accused would be saved. Such is the importance of a person's life; there is more to something than just what you believe you may have heard, and rather than giving too much credence to one's own ears, it is preferable to say that you heard nothing; this could be done without shame, given that Moses was the first to demonstrate the wisdom of speaking this way.

The account Mark gives us of Jesus' trial makes very clear allusion to this tradition; the chief priest expressly refers to it when he addresses the other members of the Sanhedrin: "You have heard the blasphemy. What do you think?" The question posed opens the door wide to all these faithful successors to Moses, who could now respond, with indeed "the agreement of the Highest," "We heard nothing!" This is a beautiful tradition, which enables the Father still to hope in the clemency of the Sanhedrin.

It is very sure that the Most High will give his agreement and even blessing to those who respond in this way to the chief priest. This is what he is waiting for from them, what he hopes for from them, and what he desires to hear from them.


## A Sorrowful Silence

I do not know how much time the rulers of the people took to reflect on their decision, to weigh in the scales the life of the man who was in

---

1. To fully appreciate the point of this, a careful reading of the passage in Leviticus is necessary and particularly v. 14, which specifies that "all that heard him" are needed to make the charge stick. (Trans.)

their hands; but they did give their reply, on which Mark prefers not to dwell, sorrowful as it is for him. "They all considered him worthy of death" (14:64). There was not one exception; it is indeed "all" who decided this way concerning the life of the Well-Beloved Son.

What measureless pain for the Father, whose hope is crushed with one blow, as is the trust he had placed in us all.

What pain for the Son, joining with his Father in the same pain.

There is silence from the Son, united with the Father, who is silent too.

A sorrowful, pained silence; not one of them has had respect for the Well-Beloved Son.

Jesus had been right in his parable of the vineyard and its tenants!

Then, as if to rub in their lack of respect, certain ones of them, Mark tells us, spit on Christ and others slap him.

Each gob of spit which soils the face of the Son, soils the heart of the Father!

Each slap which humiliates the Son, humiliates the Father.

The Holy Spirit gently drops into our hearts the words from the servant's song: "He was afflicted and oppressed, but he opened not his mouth; like a lamb that was led to the slaughter, or as a sheep before her shearers is dumb, so he opened not his mouth" (Isa 53:7).

Lord Jesus Christ, Son of God, have pity on us, sinners!

# CHAPTER 5

# Before Pilate

A S WE CONTINUE, OUR hearts attentive to the Father during the Passion of the Son, we need to pause over this new episode: the judgment before Pilate. We will again discover the presence of the Father, silent and extremely discreet, as is his custom. God is a Father who nevertheless does allow himself to intervene very discreetly—in a hidden way, hidden even from the gospel writers. It is revealed only to one of them, not to Luke as in the case of the angel's appearance, but this time to Matthew, who records a dream given to Pilate's wife.

God's intervention is so discreet that the dream takes up just one verse, the same as the angel's appearance had occupied. Here is what Matthew tells us: "While Pilate was sitting on the tribunal, his wife sent to him, saying, 'Have nothing to do with that just man, because today I have suffered many things in a dream on his account'" (27:19).

Before we consider this dream, we need to be sure we agree that God was its instigator, that it was indeed him who birthed it in the heart of this woman; to Matthew in his gospel this is an obvious fact. Indeed, in this gospel all the dreams come from God, whether those given to Joseph the carpenter on four occasions (1:20. 2:13, 19, 22), or to the wise men from the east (2:12).

As a preamble, we will consider the trial before Pilate as a whole, in the light of biblical thought.

## A Gentile Trial

When Matthew tells us that the religious leaders handed Jesus over to Pilate (27:2), we need to understand that they were handing him over to a pagan gentile,[1] to a gentile tribunal, and to the gentile law. As Jesus himself had announced to his disciples: "The chief priests and the scribes will deliver the Son of Man to the gentiles" (20:19). Earlier, when Jesus said that he would be "handed over to men" (17:22), this does not mean the same as being "handed over to the gentiles." We need to see the distinction between "men" and "gentiles."

In biblical thought, as in Jesus' thought, "men" designates the whole of humanity, in its entirety, both Israel and the other nations; these last were considered the "gentiles." To put things a little differently, "men" includes those who were open to God as well as those shut off from him, those who live with God and those who live without him. The "gentiles" are those without God, not because God has no interest in them, but because they either ignore him or are shut off from him.

There is God's world, and there is the world without God; there is the law of God and the law without God, the people of God and the people without God, the logic of God and logic without God. This is not some Manichean dichotomy,[2] but a double reality in which we all find ourselves, because there is always within each of us a pagan gentile, whether slumbering or not.

In the course of his Passion, Jesus is handed over to men, first to Israel and then to the Gentiles, first to the Sanhedrin and then to the Roman tribunal. Before the Sanhedrin, Jesus had been condemned to death; what will his fate be now, before the gentile court?

---

1. In French, the word used for Gentiles corresponds to our word pagan; each time the word "gentiles" is used here it has the thought of "pagan" behind it, as indeed it would have had to the Jews. (Trans.)

2. A Manichean dichotomy would mean saying that one group is simply good and the other simply bad. (Trans.)

Before the Sanhedrin, God had no need to intervene because it was not necessary. The Sanhedrin, invested with an authority given by God and having divine law, knew what had to be done. The master of the vineyard had no need to intervene, not only out of respect for the tenants, but because he had confidence in them, as knowing very well what they should do.

Now, however, with a Roman tribunal, a law apart from God, a gentile judge, in a world living without him, what would God do? Would he intervene? And if he did, wouldn't this be meddling in a world which carries on and functions without him; that is, would he not be infringing on human liberty?

## The Father's Discretion

In Matthew's gospel account, we find that God will indeed intervene, but with great discretion, very gently, close to the edge of but not imposing on human liberty. He will humbly knock at the door of one particular heart, with the one hope of bringing a little divine clemency to the trial of his Son. Very discreetly he knocks at the door of the heart of a person who is not a member of the tribunal but who will doubtless freely convey whatever she thinks good to the judge; that is, he approaches Pilate's wife. God could not have chosen better because she is close to Pilate but without being able to sit alongside him, in accordance with Roman law. Pilate is "sat in the judgment seat," but she is not. There is nothing she can say directly, but she can send him a message by some third party, and even this is done discreetly, because she has no place interfering in the session. We see that the woman is as discreet as God is in his dealing with her. She retains perfect freedom to do whatever she wishes with the dream God has given her; thus, her sovereign liberty is respected by God!

God, then, intervenes discreetly in the heart of this woman by means of a dream. In the dream he remains constantly hidden, very humble, revealing nothing of himself, nothing of his fatherhood, nothing of his bond of love with his Son, nothing of the Son's divinity, nothing except one short piece of information: Jesus is "a just man." Not that he is a just God, but a just man; simply that, a just man and not even "the" just, the only just one among men. No, simply a just man. It is wonderful to see how discreet God is and how he in no way forces an entrance into the woman's heart; she is quite free to reject the dream, forget it or not speak of it to anyone.

The woman receives the dream with its information about Jesus and begins to think that something strange, out of the ordinary, unaccustomed, perhaps even of great importance, is taking place at the tribunal. She sees that her husband, who she knows well enough to be aware that he is not a just man, is judging one who is just. She understands that the God who gave her this information in the dream must certainly be an unseen witness to the trial, during which an unjust man will pass judgment on a just! The woman is troubled, agitated, and fearful, so she hurries to send someone to warn her husband about what is going on—of the gravity of the situation—leaving him free to do whatever he wishes with the information. His sovereign liberty is respected by God.

For us it is easy to understand the importance of the dream. It is given to the woman to induce Pilate to be merciful, indulgent and very attentive, as one should be with a just person. In this way, the Father seeks to soften his Son's ordeal. We have it revealed to us how the Father is following his Son step by step through his Passion; how he never takes his eyes off him for one moment; how much, quite simply, he loves him. And all the time he respects the liberty of those for whom the Son is giving his life.

## "Have nothing to do with that just man"

The calamity here is that the woman conveys the contents of the dream to Pilate at the same time as she immediately and decisively closes her heart to God. She advises her husband to keep his distance, not that he show mercy, leave the hearing, or dismiss the charge. She calls on her husband to keep his distance, and this seems strange when we consider the huge distance there already was between these two, the just and the unjust. I believe that she could have told her husband not so much to leave his role to God as to ask God to step in, to come between him and Jesus, alongside him, and to help him in his conduct of the hearing. God alone can give an unjust man the light necessary to judge a just man.

What, however, does the woman say? "Have nothing to do with that just man!" This "nothing" is terrible! One might have hoped for, "Let God deal with you and that just man!" That would have been the logic of the dream: "Let God deal with you and that just man because he is your only help in this mess!" No, she says, "Have nothing to do . . ." Nothing: the word has great importance to the woman and is strongly underscored in the Greek by the fact that it is the first word out of her mouth: "Nothing to do with that just man." This "nothing" which replaces God is the sign of the radical closure of the woman against God, to whom she had opened the door a little, if only during her dream. This shutting down is also the position she asks her husband to adopt in the affair.

## A Sad Silence

The closure of self against God is such that the dream turns into a nightmare, and the trial also turns that way. Pilate has Christ scourged, and condemns him to die on a cross. God's discreet attempt to bring a little mercy to bear on the verdict has failed. After the intervention of Pilate's wife, the trial proceeds without God. Pilate exculpates himself in the washing of his hands, but the verdict is unchanged. He could have abstained from having the condemned man flogged, but he didn't. The whole trial unfolds with God excluded.

What infinite sorrow for the Father who stands in silence at the door of a human tribunal from which he is shut out, a tribunal which has condemned his Son to death!

What infinite sorrow for the Father who stands in silence at the door of a woman's heart which is closed to him, a heart that doesn't wish to be touched by him.

What infinite sorrow for the Father who stands in silence at the door of a judge's heart, a judge who washes his hands and commands the Son to be flogged; a judge who washes his hands, but cannot wash his heart.

What infinite sorrow for the Father who remains silent to receive the silent prayer of his precious Son, who has been judged, whipped and condemned to die on a cross.

The Father keeps his silence, and suffers without speaking of it to anyone, except for the grieved dove who has found no place to alight in these closed hearts.

What humble love, suffering in secret.

What infinite sorrow for the Son, judged in this way, flogged, condemned to be crucified . . . and yet saying nothing, finding refuge in the silence of prayer and the silence of his Father, in humble and deep communion of love with him.

But what sorrow also for this woman who, as she tells her husband, "suffers many things," little knowing that the just man she speaks of had announced to his disciples that he would "suffer many things" (16:21). It is exactly the same expression, except that the woman suffers in a heart that she has closed to God, while Christ suffers in a heart which he has opened to all. The Father suffers doubly, in compassion for the suffering of this woman and his Son.

The consolation for the Father is to know that his Son is still standing tall, despite the flogging and the death sentence; his Son is still upright in silent prayer, always upright, strengthened by what he received from the angel in the garden.

> The consolation of the Son is the infinite love of his Father . . .
> May you be praised, humble Comforter, Holy Spirit,
> you who perform in secret your work of tenderness
> in the heart of the Father and the heart of the Son!

"Pilate handed Jesus over to them to be crucified" (27:26). Such is the outcome of human logic, logic without God.

Two days previously, Jesus had said to his disciples, "the Son of Man will be delivered up to be crucified" (26:2). In saying this, Jesus blends two contrary forms of reason, each as "foolish" as the other: on one hand, the logic of men, foolish enough to conclude in the condemnation of the Son to death on a cross; on the other, the logic of God, foolish enough to conclude in the Son giving his life for men on the same cross for their salvation. The logic of men is pursued from one tribunal to the next, and the logic of God is also being pursued, mysteriously, through this same human reasoning which nevertheless shuts him out.

Pilate condemns Jesus to the cross, reaching the very height of folly of a world without God, little knowing that he is in fact bringing to pass God's own logic, which is also reaching its height. God's foolishness—this other foolishness, not that of man in his rejection of God—is that of God in his love for man.

Christ now leaves the tribunal, his heart grieved by the lack of love of a world which lives without God; he leaves, his heart full of his Father's love for this world for which he is giving his life.

We will also leave, enveloped in his love! We will accompany the Lord on his way to the cross with a view to entering a little more deeply into the humble and holy love of God.

May he bless us and lead us!

# CHAPTER 6

# Simon of Cyrene

After Luke, to whom the revelation was given of the angel in Gethsemane, and after Matthew, who tells us about the dream of Pilate's wife, it is now Mark's turn to receive a similar gift; and it is again with the goal of opening our hearts to the endless mystery of the Father's presence and to his inexpressible love for his Son throughout the ordeal of the Passion. So we now turn our attention to Mark's gospel.

The episode which relates Simon's involvement on the way to the cross is only found in the first three gospels. John's interests did not embrace the presence of this man and we can understand why; Jesus alone is at the heart of his concerns and meditation, to such a degree that finally he only sees him and pays no attention to those around him. It is as if these others were stars, always present but never seen once the sun has risen. John has eyes only for Jesus, so great is his love for him.

In the first three gospels the place accorded Simon is very limited, taking up just one verse: in Matthew (27:32), in Luke (23:26), as in Mark (15:21). Here is what Mark says: "They (the soldiers) compelled a passer-by, one Simon of Cyrene, coming up out of the country, the father of Alexander and Rufus, to carry his cross."

There is just this one verse, with regard to which there are two possibilities; either the presence of Simon is of little importance and merited no more, or on the other hand it is of such great importance that it contains something of mystery beyond words. The greater a mystery, the fewer the words there are to express it!

The presence of Simon with Jesus is not of a fleeting, fugitive nature. Certainly not! By this I mean that the time spent with him was relatively long; it may be difficult to determine exactly how long, but it must have been the whole length of the route from the time they left the Praetorium right up to the summit of Golgotha—several hundred meters. There's no doubt this cannot have represented just a few minutes, not when we consider that they would have covered the distance at the speed of a man condemned to death!

This entire trajectory or pathway is the subject of just the one verse. This concision is indeed out of the ordinary, and I believe it invites us to read the verse allowing time to unfold before us, pondering Christ at length as if we were following the same route ourselves; following the steps of the condemned man, allowing ourselves to open up little by little to the mystery of Christ on his way to the cross.

In order to signal the importance of the passage towards Golgotha and the sorrow that weighs around it, Luke takes time to mention the presence of certain women weeping, their hearts bleeding to see the condemned man pass by, considered innocent as he is by so many. This gives Luke the opportunity to underline the importance of the tears, and to tell us Jesus' response to the women: "Daughters of Jerusalem, don't weep for me, but weep for yourselves and your children . . . !" (23:28). This extraordinary response of Christ to these "daughters of Jerusalem" immediately induces the women so named by Jesus to look at him in a new way, and actually to redouble their tears for him. Who is this condemned man who speaks to them as only the well-beloved of the Song of Songs had ever done, calling out to the inhabitants of the holy city (Song 2:7, 3:5, 8:4)?[1] Here he is, the one who is love-sick, who roams the streets of Jerusalem looking for his well-beloved, now treading the same streets on his way to be crucified!

---

1. The point is that the phrase occurs only in these two places. (Trans.)

## A Silent Pathway

However, we will not dwell on this particular occurrence since it is not Mark's interest. For him, the progress to Golgotha unfolds in perfect silence, and I would actually say a particularly strong silence. From the guardhouse to Golgotha the silence is complete although the whole world is there! Almost all the people who were at the trial are going to re-gather at Golgotha; they are following the same route, but saying nothing, not so much as opening their mouths, while the condemned man advances. Sometimes there are scenes of such gravity that they impose silence on the witnesses; this is what Mark and Matthew underline by the brevity of their one verse accounts, simple verses full of a deep, dense silence.

I have used the word "silence" here in a singular form, but it is clear that this silence includes a plurality of silences, as different as the various people along the way to the cross. Please follow me, reader friend, as I depict these different silences each with its peculiarity, and ponder the mosaic of silence which will help us grasp the unusual beauty of God's silence.

The order in which we consider them is of little importance. It is not chronological; all the silences intermingle, all along the route to Golgotha. This is how the way of the cross of our Lord unfolds—in an array of silences that border on the indescribable, blending together into one, into a dense mystery, which it is difficult to represent.

## The Soldiers' Silence

We will think first about the soldiers, since they would have occupied center-front stage, and they would have been the last to have spoken when still in the courtyard of the Praetorium. What they had then said was particularly painful to hear, wounding to Jesus as it all was. We are not talking about one single disrespectful soldier but of a cohort, six hundred soldiers when complete, though this would not have been the case in this instance. At all events, there were dozens and dozens of soldiers abandoning themselves to mockery or even obscenity, pouring it all out on Christ; and Christ in the middle of them says nothing. He undergoes this, unable to offer the least resistance. What pain for him, and also for us to be witnesses of it.

Then we see them leave the barracks, and the soldiers requisition Simon of Cyrene, who just happens to be passing by on his way in from the country; and then suddenly there is silence, an amazing silence which must have been a tremendous relief to Jesus—silence at last! Finally the yelling has stopped, all the wounding mockery and the tumult of the soldiery.

When Jesus leaves the Praetorium, the soldiers leave with him and accompany him right up to the place of torture, where we will re-join and listen to them again later, once Jesus has been put on the cross. Notably, we will examine the moment when Jesus is presented vinegar to drink and the figure of Elijah is invoked to taunt him (15:36). But before that, between the Praetorium and the hill of Golgotha, the soldiers are silent, perhaps on the look-out for incursions from the crowd—who knew, with this pretend king, perhaps he might have partisans who, if necessary, would need containing or suppressing?

## The Crowd's Silence

The crowd of people is not named as such in our short verse, but they too are clearly present along the way. They were there during the trial before Pilate; they will be there again at the cross; and they too are following along the way.

If we speak of the crowd's collective silence, it is in contrast with the way they act before Pilate and again at the cross. What Mark reports about them before Pilate is remarkable. Mark tells us that when the crowd was questioned by Pilate they began "to cry out" (15:13), and when questioned further began to "cry out beyond measure" (*perissōs*), as he specifies (v. 14). The cries of the crowd not only rise to a crescendo but reach greater heights still, "beyond all measure." What the crowd says is limited to just two words of extreme violence, "Crucify him!" (vv. 13 and 14). These cries are driven like nails into Jesus' heart.

Once at the foot of the cross the crowd begins to interfere again, and what is said is considered by Mark to consist of blasphemies;[2] "the passers-by blasphemed," he tells us, reporting their words, which could not but wound Jesus again (v. 29).

Between the cries and shouts of the tribunal and the curses of Golgotha, the crowd is silent, all along the route, a silence as welcome to Jesus as that of the soldiers.

The crowd is not mentioned by Mark as being there along the way to the cross; he is silent on the matter. This should alert us to the fact that a person passed over in silence . . . is not necessarily absent. You will understand, reader friend, that this remark would refer also to the Father, no doubt every bit as present as the crowd, and just as silent.

## Other Silences

We could say the same thing about the two thieves,[3] of whom Mark doesn't speak until the moment of the crucifixion (v. 27), not troubling to mention that they too, condemned to the same punishment as Jesus, had followed the same route and at the same time. Luke indeed is careful to specify this; "at the same time, two malefactors were led out to be put to death with Jesus" (23:32). Here again, Mark's silence about them along the way to Golgotha does not indicate their absence; it simply shows that Mark is focusing all his attention, and ours, on Simon and Jesus.

---

**2.** The French word can equally mean blasphemy or cursing. (Trans.)

**3.** A detailed and very fine discussion of the two thieves may be found in the author's book *From Darkness to Light.* (Trans.)

The thieves were ever present; Luke tells us that they spoke up when they were nailed to their crosses, but along the way to Golgotha their silence is a fact, and it joins the other silences.

Mary, the mother of our Lord, and also John, the beloved disciple, are there, as we learn from John's gospel (19:25). The two are silent at the foot of the cross, and we can suppose them already silently present along the way there; perhaps they were in tears like the daughters of Jerusalem, silently flowing tears which merge into the profound silence of the scene.

There are also certain women who Mark notes at the foot of the cross, some of whose names he carefully records: Mary Magdalene, Mary the mother of James, Salome, and others besides (15:40–41). All of these women who had followed Jesus up from Galilee, silent at the foot of the cross, were also silent along the way to Golgotha. No one will ever know of how many tears the women's silence is composed, but a verse from Lamentations rises in my heart: "All you who pass by, look and see if there be any sorrow like my sorrow . . ." (1:12)

## Simon's Silence

It may be that we are losing focus; where Mark is much more sober, I am becoming long-winded. The list of unnamed people along the roadside is long, but we should now stick to what Mark says, as he concentrates everything into the one verse flooded with silence, leading us to ponder the only two on whom his attention is fixed, Simon and Jesus.

This is the moment, then, to look at Simon and underline how remarkable his silence is, and how loudly it speaks to us. Everything about him invites us to silence, immerses us in silence and leads us back to silence.

Even his name makes of him a being of silence; Simon means, "one who listens." How wonderful! In order to listen, you have to be silent; we see this man was born for silence, consecrated to silence by the name he received. He is a being of silence, a silence that listens.

"He was coming out of the countryside," Mark tells us. No doubt he had listened to the birds singing in the fields that morning, in the quiet of budding trees, of opening flowers and the sun drinking up the morning dew.

Simon has left the silence of the country this morning to instead be listening to the crowd in the streets of Jerusalem, when suddenly he finds himself required by the soldiers to carry a cross not destined for him, beside a condemned man unknown to him, and in whom he discovers nothing but silence. Simon has listened carefully to this condemned man along the length of their painful path, but hears never a word from his mouth; then he has listened to his silence, because silence can speak; it said, "like a lamb that is dumb, being led to the slaughter" (Isa 53:7). Did the silence perhaps speak to Simon like this? I prefer to think so, Simon being a Jew. We don't know if he knew the Scriptures well, but he would have known enough for this verse to come to mind along the way to Golgotha. This condemned fellow "has no beauty or form that we should desire him" (53:2) and is indeed "like a lamb that is dumb . . ." The route to Golgotha, through the streets of the holy city, is long enough to allow Simon time to meditate on what the silence says to him as he meditates a few verses of Scripture.

Having left the silence of the country that morning, Simon will not open his mouth or address even one word to his silent neighbor, and will leave to the same silence. There is no more mention of him in the New Testament; he is a man we know nothing of barring this one day, and that barely for an hour or so. His name appears nowhere else in the Bible; for us, he disappears into the depths of God's heart. He was born to listen. He listened to the silence of Jesus and perhaps finished his days treasuring in his heart the sound of that silence, similar perhaps to the "sound of silence" which filled Elijah's heart in the cave on Mount Horeb (1 Kgs 19:12). Never would Simon be able to forget or cease to sound the bottomless depth of silence of that condemned man on that morning; it was a silence with the savor of God.

Nobody will know if my tentative suggestion about Simon is correct because he said nothing. He kept hidden in the secret of his heart what he experienced on the way to the cross. But for me, reader friend, he will always be a man who bears much thinking about because nobody was closer to Jesus that day. Nobody else has experienced the grace of carrying, not his own cross, as each disciple is called to do, but that of Jesus, the very cross of Jesus, united to him by that cross, united to him in the pain of physical effort; and also united with him, mysteriously, by the silence, from the time they leave the guardroom courtyard right up to the top of Golgotha, in the steps of this man condemned to death.

Blessed be God for giving us Simon.

## The Silence of the Scriptures

In the long list of silences which intersect and mingle in this one short verse so heavy with meaning, we need to consider another strange silence, that of the Scriptures. By this I mean that the Scriptures say nothing, make no announcement or prophecy about this episode in the Passion.

You will have noticed that through the length of the Passion the evangelists are careful to enumerate all the prophecies, one by one, as they are fulfilled, from the day of Tabernacles up to the Paschal morning and on to the well-known moment in particular when the Resurrected One, after rejoining his disciples, opens the Scriptures to them, showing them everything that concerned him from Moses to the prophets, including the Psalms (Luke 24:44). The four evangelists were at pains to mention each successive event when they composed their gospel accounts: the parting of Jesus' clothes at the foot of the cross (Matt 27:35), Jesus' side pierced by the lance (John 19:34, 37), and so many other details which are reported as fulfilling Scripture. Nevertheless, there is nothing about Simon in Mark or any other gospel. This is what I mean by the silence of the Scriptures.

I have gone to considerable trouble to discover if, through his choice of words in this verse, Mark might have left or made some allusion, more or less discreet, or if perhaps there was some episode or verse in the Scriptures, but it was fruitless trouble! Cyrene is passed over totally in silence in the Old Testament although the town was already 700 years old and the book of Acts tells us there was a synagogue there (6:9).

The verb "requisition," so strikingly used about Simon, is unknown in the Old Testament, as are all its derivatives. Furthermore, nobody in the Old Testament "comes out of the country," as we are told of Simon. Finally, there is the lack of any allusion even to the word "cross," which the Old Testament ignores. Mark might have used the word "tree" which would have referred back to an article of the law in Deuteronomy concerning those condemned to "hang on a tree"; this would have been particularly illuminating with the regard to the Passion. But Mark prefers the word "cross" and so makes no reference to any scriptural text.

All this leads me to believe that Simon emerges out of the silence of the Scriptures. It seems to be that the Scriptures intend to shroud him in mystery. And yet he was so close to Jesus, so united to him in silence, as if Mark had intended to wrap Simon and Jesus up together in the silence, a deep and silent mystery.

Jesus, as we have seen, had been at pains to announce to his disciples over and over again that he had to die; these announcements went so far at times as to give particular details, that he would be spat upon and mocked (Mark 10:34), as well as important matters like Peter's denial (14:30), or Judas's betrayal (14:1). In none of these accounts, though, is there the least allusion to the passage of events concerning Simon. It looks as though Jesus also wished for this moment, important nonetheless, to be kept in the silence of mystery.

Who is this Simon Cyrene, stepping out of the early morning silence and returning to the silence shortly afterwards, without so much as making the sound of his voice heard? It is indeed a mystery!

## Jesus' Silence

Now we turn to Jesus, whose silence overtops that of everyone else and particularly captures our attention. We have said that things are a little different in Luke's gospel, where we find the encounter with the "daughters of Jerusalem" which proves an occasion for Jesus to speak; in Mark, however, the entire route from the guardhouse to Golgotha is covered wordlessly. Simon and Jesus are united in silence. We should note that before the encounter with Simon, Jesus was already silent, and that his silence had not passed unnoticed. Before the soldiers in the barracks' precincts, during the farce of dressing him as king (15:17); then, as he sustained the blows with which they struck him as well as the spitting which humiliated him (v. 19); throughout all of this, Jesus is totally silent, without so much as responding to those who nevertheless spoke to him, saying, "Hail, King of the Jews" (v. 18).

Still earlier, before the Roman tribunal, Jesus had only responded to Pilate's first question ("Are you the king of the Jews?" 15:2), and had then become silent and never ceased to be so until he was on the cross. Jesus' silence at the tribunal had astonished Pilate, who even questioned him about it: "Do you not reply?" (15:4). Mark adds a comment here, and this further pricks our ears: "Jesus made no reply, which amazed Pilate" (v. 5). This amazing silence is remarked by Pilate as well as by Mark.

Still earlier, before the Sanhedrin, as we saw, Jesus had adopted the same attitude as before Pilate. When the false witnesses had made their depositions against Jesus without eliciting the slightest response, the high priest had been astounded and cried out, "Do you make no reply?" (14:60), to which Mark himself adds: "He kept silence and replied not a word!" (v. 61).

Such is the attitude adopted by Jesus. Silence appears to have been a veritable refuge for him; he would step back into it given the least occasion, perhaps as a sanctified space in which to pray. I think everything we discover in Mark's gospel inclines us in this direction; silence was for Jesus a place of prayer. If, then, Jesus kept silence all the way to Golgotha, it is because all the way there, he was praying. Every step on the way of the cross is for him a step of prayer.

Mark himself reports Jesus' first words after reaching Golgotha, when he was on the cross: "My God, my God, why have you forsaken me?" (15:34). These words are a prayer; after this, continuing to look just at Mark's gospel, Jesus says nothing more until the loud cry at the moment he dies (v. 37). Clearly, Jesus had held to prayer as his recourse in the face of death, and the prayer uttered on the cross stems from the long journey to get there, which was already one long prayer, silent prayer.

It seems to me that this is what Peter too understood when he writes in his first letter that when Jesus "was reviled, he reviled not again; when he suffered he threatened not, but committed himself to him that judges righteously" (2:23). I understand that in the context of the Passion, to "commit oneself" in this way to God (*paradidōmi*) means to "commit oneself, entrust oneself to him in prayer."

Alongside Simon, Jesus was praying, preparing himself for death; no doubt in his silent prayer he also prayed for the crowd, for the soldiers, for the thieves and for Simon. It was silent prayer of such intensity that it drew in behind him everyone who saw him immersed in this deep silence, inviting them too to be silent and perhaps to pray.

Simon was the closest person to Jesus along the way and so was best placed to understand this praying silence of Jesus; this is why, it seems to me, he respected his silence and didn't intrude on it; he said nothing. When one is alongside someone who is praying in silence, this is both seen and felt, and the need to be silent oneself becomes obvious.

This is what Simon does. He carries the cross of the condemned man, who prays in silence as they advance towards the place of death.

Blessed Simon, for hearing the praying silence of Jesus and participating in it. Blessed Simon, walking in the steps of such a man of prayer. Blessed Simon, following in the furrow of prayer plowed by Jesus.

Simon has joined his silent prayer to that of Jesus. Proceeding with Simon along the way of the cross and relieved of the full weight of the cross, Jesus is surely thankful for his companion in prayer. We too are there in silence, watching Jesus and Simon joined in the mystery of shared prayer.

At the foundation of the world, the Spirit of God hovered in silence over the great deep, and the dove hovers in silence now over the endless mystery of a man united with Christ in the bond of prayer.

This shared prayer of Simon and Jesus would be turned surely only towards God, whose own silence now seems particularly striking. God's silence mingles with all the silences we have enumerated; it's his we will next consider, having examined those of the soldiers, the crowd, the thieves, the women, and of Simon and Jesus.

The silence of the condemned man's prayer as he goes towards the place of torture is the silence of the Son's prayer on his way to the cross, within the silence of the Father. On this we now need to dwell; what should we say of the Father during the long silence of the condemned man's march, the march of the Son, from the barracks to Golgotha's hill? Our brief verse from the gospel, so packed and full of silences, also has in it the surprising mystery of the silent presence of the Father.

## The Father's Silence

It leaps out from the gospels of Mark and Luke in particular, that throughout his baptism in the Jordan Jesus maintained total silence, and Luke specifies that it was the silence of prayer (3:21). It's in that silence that Jesus hears a word of love from his Father, a word which strengthens his heart through the course of his ministry and in particular to face the ordeal of the temptation in the wilderness immediately following the baptism.

Jesus is now approaching Golgotha to face the ordeal of death, and he had told his disciples that this death would be for him a new baptism: "I have a baptism to be baptized with, and how long it is in its accomplishment!" (Luke 12:50).[4] Would this perhaps mean that in the prayerful silence along the way of the cross, Jesus was listening for some new word of love from his Father, or for some sign from him? It is certainly within the realms of possibility. All the time along the way of the cross, Jesus only prayed, prayer which plainly was open to the love of his Father.

Mark tells us that following the baptism in the Jordan, angels came to silently serve Jesus, to help him face the ordeal of temptation (1:13). Would angels come once again to Jesus' side, perhaps just one, to serve him and prepare him to face the ordeal of death?

We saw in Gethsemane how the Father said nothing, but sent a silent angel who strengthened Jesus. Would the strength he then received—the strength of humble love given by the Father—suffice to see him through death? Would the Father need to give the Son some extra strength for the final struggle?

Reader friend, all these questions jostle each other in my heart and flow from my meditation of the gospels as I ponder Christ on the way of his cross. Whether or not these are good or false questions, I am not sure, but I ask the Lord once more to open the Scriptures to me and to open my heart if only a little; to open to me the mystery of the Father's love for the Son, this mystery which is hidden away deep in the Scriptures.

---

4. "How long" is the French rendition; "oppressed" or "afflicted" is closer to the Greek; "straightened" in KJV is very good.(Trans.)

O Holy Spirit, Spirit of the Father and of the Son, please come in your grace to open the Scriptures, which you yourself inspired, and come to open my heart!

## Simon, the Father of Alexander and Rufus

Turning back once more to Mark's short verse devoted to Simon, my attention is drawn to an expression, reader friend, which we have not previously examined. It is found only in Mark: "Simon, the father of Alexander and Rufus." I searched for a long time to find why Mark should give us this piece of information revealing the existence of these two well-known unknowns, Alexander and Rufus! No mention is made of either of them in the rest of the New Testament, so why speak of them? Why overburden the otherwise so concise text with irrelevant detail? There are other, much more important things to say which would throw light on Simon's presence alongside Jesus. There is indeed a Rufus mentioned by Paul in one of his letters (Rom 16:13), but this is a Rufus who lives in Rome and is cited in connection with his mother, not Simon. Speaking of Rufus from Rome is like speaking of Marcel from Marseilles!

My thinking bumped up against the two names of these unknowns for a long time and in vain until my attention shifted onto the first word in Mark's phrase, not Alexander and Rufus, but the word "father": "Simon, the father of Alexander and Rufus." At this point things became clear, and I still weep for joy in the light that pours from this insight.

The light came because it is absolutely unique in the Bible that a man be introduced in this way. The ancient biblical custom, which has never been abandoned to this day in Israel, was always to identify a man by presenting him in relation to his father. Thus, James the son of Alphaeus (Mark 3:17), Judas the son of Simon (John 13:2), Bartimaeus the son of Timaeus (Mark 10:46) and so many others; the list is endless, not only in the gospels but in the rest of the New Testament and throughout the Old. The custom was so anchored in their hearts that it was even possible to omit the word "son" and to say just "James of Zebedee" (Mark 3:17) and everyone would know that this meant James the son of Zebedee; this can be confirmed with a little digging into the Bible—our translators have needed to add in the word "son."

In a way that is exceptional for the Bible, then, things are handled differently here; Mark presents Simon not as "the son of" but as "the father of." Why should there be this exception, this originality? Why go against tradition? Why, if not to make something new be understood, something so radical that Mark dares not go too far because in saying it he opens the door to a deep mystery! Such a substantial mystery cannot be more than suggested and implanted in us for prayer deep in our contemplative mind. In the divine self-hiding this secret is revealed to Mark alone of the evangelists, in the same way it led to the Gethsemane angel being revealed only to Luke, and the dream of Pilate's wife only to Matthew.

What then is this secret I am so hesitant to speak of it, reader friend, fearful as I am of being clumsy and spoiling its great and humble beauty? May the Lord forgive me if I touch his endless modesty!

## The Presence of the Father

Mark is suggesting that the man who is carrying the cross of Jesus is a father, and that he has the care of a father for the condemned man, the heart of a father, the compassion of a father. He is there in the silence of a father as a paternal presence, so that for Christ it is his Father who is drawing near to him in this simple human father, humbly and invisibly in the visible man, silently in this man of silence, sustaining him through the sustenance of this man, measuring his steps to Jesus' and so bearing his cross.

The hidden presence of God through the father of Alexander and Rufus is what throws such an inexpressible light on this verse.

What an endless mystery! It is invisible to our poor eyes, which see only Simon and Jesus. This unseen mystery takes place in such a deep silence that I understand why the soldiers said nothing, the crowd neither, nor the thieves, no one—they can feel it without understanding. Heaven and earth were silent.

This is not an angel descending from heaven to strengthen Christ, but infinitely more in that it is infinitely more hidden, more humble; it is the Father himself invisibly drawing near, and in this man of flesh and blood he comes to carry the cross of his Son, and all in silence. Reader friend, this is the Father's silence during the Passion, a silence of infinite beauty which merges with all the other silences, concealed in them and going far beyond them. Such is the presence of the Father during the Passion of the Son, a hidden presence, hidden here for a while in the presence of a man, one Simon, the father of Alexander and Rufus.

## The Hidden Presence

Did Simon feel or understand something of what was taking place through him? I know nothing! I believe it was not so, without being able to allow myself to absolutely affirm it. Who am I to say? It is certainly true that Simon never said anything, never ventured beyond his silence, and I prefer to leave him tenderly in the silence of his bond with God. We know very well, reader friend, how it can be that one person is a manifestation of God to another; this can happen quite unwittingly, which is how it is best left. God is wiser than we are and is unwilling to compromise what little humility there might be in our hearts! Undoubtedly, this is how it was with Simon; he was a manifestation of the Father for the Son, not through the course of life, but for the time along the route to the cross, from the guardhouse precincts to the hill of Golgotha.

For Christ, however, what did this mean? He is God himself, so much so that nothing of God is hidden from him. This is fact; but in his humanity, what did he perceive of God's hidden presence? It is very difficult to say; the whole mystery of Christ's humanity is here, inseparable though it is from his divinity. I believe, however, that in his humanity he received in the silence of his prayer the ability to perceive this presence as he had always been able; as he said to his disciples, "I am not alone, the Father is with me" (John 16:32).

At the Jordan, the Father spoke to the Son. Here, nothing is said, but this is more effective; his active presence speaks louder than any words.

## And the Holy Spirit

If the Father and the Son are together in this, what of the Holy Spirit? This is a good question to ask, believing as we do that the Trinity is indivisible. The Holy Spirit is so humble that he can easily pass unnoticed; but I believe he is present, wonderfully hidden, wonderfully humble, with a humility which is active. Just as the Father works in synergy with the Son along the way to the cross, the Spirit works in concert with Mark in the secret of his heart and nudges him to write in this way what he certainly wouldn't have written of himself. So it is that Mark and the Holy Spirit wrote together, "Simon, the father of Alexander and Rufus." The Spirit works in this way in Mark's heart through the discreet power of persuasion; this is inspiration. Mark writes with all his heart, all his conviction, all his faith, opening himself to the Spirit who comes stealing into his heart, intent on revealing to him a little of the mystery of the measureless love of the Father for the Son. This is how Mark writes and, as he does, ponders what the Spirit has given him to write; he ponders the Father through the father of

Alexander and Rufus; he ponders the Father and the Son bearing the cross along the way to Golgotha.

However, the Spirit doesn't stop here. He continues to pursue his work in us, enabling us too to ponder the Father and the Son bearing the cross on the way to Golgotha.

If the Holy Spirit led Mark to ponder the mystery in this way, it was to open it up before us too, as discreetly as possible, thereby guarding the mystery of the humble and modest love of the Father for the Son.

It might be that in our hearts we begin to resist or even rebel against this. What connection, after all, could there be between God, the Totally Other, and a simple man from small-town Cyrene who happens along near the barracks as he comes up from the country? Reader friend, it is a connection that goes way beyond my understanding, but I believe the Holy Spirit breathed this into Mark's heart and led him to compose this passage of the gospel for our edification. I also believe that the Father, in his infinite love for the Son, thought it good to proceed this way, to work so humbly through a man; and my heart marvels at this. I marvel to contemplate the Totally Other, incorporeal and invisible, making himself known through a visible flesh-and-blood man. I marvel at such a Father, who is our Father too; I marvel to see him act like this, the invisible through the visible, the imperceptible through the perceptible, the incomprehensible through the comprehensible, the eternal through the temporal. His humble love, his divine love can manifest through human love, his compassion through the compassion of a Simon for a condemned man, his divine fatherhood through the father of Alexander and Rufus.

Reader friend, it is a good thing to be silent for a while and take time to ponder this mystery.

O celestial King, Comforter, Spirit of truth, you who are everywhere present and who fill all things, treasure of goodness and giver of life, come and dwell in us; purify us from every defilement and save our souls!

## A Similar Situation _____

A similar manifestation had occurred earlier in the temple in Jerusalem at the time of Jesus' presentation as an infant, again reported in just one gospel, that of Luke. On that day, as you know, Mary and Joseph entered the temple in Jerusalem "to present the child to the Lord" (Luke 2:22), which is to say, to his heavenly Father. So, what happened? A man stepped forward, one Simeon, and this elderly man took Jesus up into his arms—not God, a man; but in this fatherly gesture of Simeon's we can readily see the Father embracing the Son (Luke 2:25–32). Again, what a measureless mystery! The elderly Simeon, emerging out of the silence and returning to silence, was a manifestation of the Father to the Son.

How, then, do we see the presence of God during the Passion? To our eyes he is invisible; however, this is not absence, but hidden presence, so humbly hidden as to be buried. It is so buried that only the Holy Spirit, who alone can "search the deep things of God" (1 Cor 2:10), was able to reveal it to a man, as he did to Mark in the composition of his gospel.

I hope this is clear enough for us, but I will repeat it, just to be sure that there can be no misunderstanding; Simon was no angel and not God, just a being of flesh and blood like us. He was not God, but a manifestation of God. An angel is a manifestation of God, but consciously so; Simon was too, but no doubt unconsciously. An angel may bring a message to transmit, as in Zacharias's case, or Mary's or the shepherds'. Simon bore none. He was not a manifestation of the Father in the eyes of the crowd or the soldiers, but for Christ alone he was, in his simple humanity.

## John's Point of View

If the Father was helping the Son bear the cross, this can help us receive a little differently what John tells us in his gospel which is silent about Simon. We need not take this as a contradictory silence, but a silence meaning that the presence of the Father with the Son was beyond description, as inexpressible as the occasions of the baptism or the transfiguration, neither of which John reports; he doesn't report the episode in Gethsemane either, although he was aware of it; instead he is content merely with referring to what Jesus said to Peter: "Shall I not drink the cup which the Father has given me to drink?" (18:11). We notice that John seems to avoid those episodes which emphasize the bond between the Father and the Son, no doubt to avoid making the indescribable too plain.

In John's gospel, then, the presence of the Father is always so inexpressible that Jesus himself doesn't speak of it except in terms which go beyond concrete description. For example, "the Father is in me and I am in the Father."

The inexpressible presence of the Father is also signposted by what Jesus says on the threshold of the Passion, words which illuminate the whole event: "I am not alone, the Father is with me" (16:32). These words of Jesus are to be understood as an affirmation of the Father's constant presence through the entire course of the Passion, including this time carrying the cross. How in this instance is the Father with the Son, united to him? It may be beyond description and speech and imagination, but this doesn't prevent it, though inexpressible, from being very real. The Father is indeed with the Son as he carries the cross, but in a way which escapes our eyes and understanding. This matches very well, though differently stated, with what arises from Mark's gospel in what he says about Simon of Cyrene.

The inexpressible will always be just that: it can only be evoked, suggested, as the Holy Spirit leads in various ways. Thus, it seems to me, Mark and John both express the inexpressible, each in his own way, as the Spirit led them.


## "Two walk together"

One point remains to be clarified, not as satisfaction for our curiosity, but to help better understand what is revealed here; our spiritual life as a whole may be illuminated as we look at the issue of our also being invited by Jesus to take up the cross. What can we say of our own cross in the light of Jesus' experience? Did the Father, in the person of Simon, carry the cross of the Son alone, or did they bear it together? We need to apply ourselves anew to the text, not just Mark's on this occasion, but the other gospels too, because much depends on Simon's exact role.

Mark tells us that Simon was requisitioned to carry Jesus' cross. The text is succinct and indecisive, leaving two readings open: we can understand either that Simon carried Jesus' cross in his place, alone, or that he carried it with him. Both are possible in terms of physical fact; the cross could be carried alone or by two. In fact, it is known today that they had only to carry the horizontal beam of the cross, as the vertical component was already fixed in the ground. Even so, the beam might have been carried by two or by one.

Matthew's text leaves us with the same double possibility. Luke, however, adds a new piece of information, telling us that Simon had to carry the cross "behind" Jesus, though this still does not resolve the ambiguity; it could be that Simon was carrying the cross alone behind Jesus, or that Simon carried it with him, one behind the other.

In John we find the answer to the difficulty. John doesn't mention the presence of Simon and says simply that "Jesus carried his cross" (19:17). Despite the absence of any mention of Simon, I believe that this makes things clear, and we can suppose that Jesus and Simon carried the cross together. This respects the four gospels; the first three become very clear, "Simon carried the cross of Jesus with him, one behind the other," and the fourth shines with the same light but with different reflections. For John, in effect, the Father is truly present on the way to Golgotha, not behind Christ but in him. In this way we see one light shining in the four gospels, with differing objectives.

This being so, if Jesus and Simon carried the cross together, we can legitimately think that the Father drew near to carry the cross with his Son, in profound synergy with him, in an intimate communion of love which fills our hearts with thanksgiving.

## To Carry the Sin of the World

The Father and the Son together carry the cross. For the expression "carry the cross" the Greek has recourse to different words, but the most frequent by far is that used here by Mark, *airō*. This word is also found in the mouth of John the Baptist as he considers "the lamb who carries the sin of the world" (John 1:29). Why link these two phrases? Quite simply, because the cross carried by Jesus is the sin of the world. In carrying the cross, Jesus bore the sin of the world which is why the cross is so heavy, with a weight beyond understanding. At the same time, the one who is carrying the sin of the world is no more than a lamb, a lamb who opens not his mouth . . . but you know the rest of the verse.

As Simon carries the cross with Jesus, he is a precious and very great support, but he doesn't carry more than one end of a piece of wood, heavy though that might be. Simon relieves Jesus of much physical effort, as the soldiers too support him, and this is really something; but we should also add in the factor of compassion, and this is wonderful too, since compassion is a real force over and above the physical, and complementary to it. This does not lessen the fact that with Simon behind him, Jesus is alone in carrying the sin of the world—truly alone. Simon carries none of this sin, no more than do we.

With regard to the Father things are different, wonderfully so, because the Father—positioning himself with the Son to carry the cross—truly bears the sin of the world with him. Indeed, the Father and the Son bear the sin of the world together, in a wonderful communion of love, of which, marvelously, we are beneficiaries.

That said, I believe it should be said once more, that any shade of sadism is dissipated in this incomparable light. The Father does not impose on the Son the task of carrying the sin of the world alone, but comes to bear it with him, and this is at the heart of our meditation and thanksgiving.

We see, reader friend, that this one small gospel verse from Mark contains an endless mystery. When we ponder this scene it is through and beyond the visible that we are able to contemplate the invisible. Beyond Simon and Jesus who tread their way together towards Golgotha, carrying the cross together, we are to contemplate the invisible in the Father and the Son, in their humble love, carrying together the sin of the world; the Father and the Son in silence, weighed down with the sin of the world.

What an infinite mystery of humble love!

The Father and the Son press forward together, step by step towards Golgotha, and we follow behind in the wake of their silence.

On that morning, the soldiers, the crowd, the thieves, the women in tears all were silent.

Today, and in God's eternity, heaven and earth bow down and are silent.

## "If anyone will come after me, let him take up his cross"

"If anyone will come after me, let him take up his cross and follow me" (Matt 16:24; Mark 8:34; Luke 9:23). As we listen to what Jesus says to his disciples, to each of us, we need to be very attentive and avoid any confusion. Jesus did not say "let him take up my cross," but "let him take up his cross." It is not Christ's cross but ours, so that we are in no sense invited to carry Jesus' cross as Simon did; no one is invited to take Simon's place, far less that of God! Simon carried Jesus' cross, certainly, but Jesus tells us to carry our cross. It is helpful to note that when Simon carried Jesus' cross, it did not become his!

Further, as we compare Jesus and ourselves, we see that the cross is not situated at the same point of our lives. For Jesus, it was at the end of his journey, at the close of his life, right at the very end, whereas for us it is to be found at the very beginning. The statement addressed to the disciples on this matter makes it very clear that the cross is a preliminary, preceding the disciple's spiritual walk, right at the beginning, as a preface to it: "if anyone will come after me, that is, become my disciple, let him begin by taking up his cross, and only then, follow me."

Finally, another important difference, reported by Luke alone, is that for Jesus the cross was a reality on the last day of his life, whereas for us, Jesus tells us that it is to be a reality of each day: "let him take up his cross daily." Thus, the cross was occasional in the life of Jesus, but becomes daily and permanent for us.

"Daily; day after day." We can cry against this as an injustice and rebel against it, which is what happens often enough.

Why should we now be speaking about this invitation of Jesus if the differences are so important and there is perhaps little in common between us? Simply because the same expression is used for him (John 19:17) and for us—"to take up the cross"—and because as well as the differences, there is also a point of contact we will do well to consider. However, we should not forget that our cross will never be his; in particular, when Jesus was carrying the cross he was carrying the sin of the world—the weight of ours will never be the same. He has never required of us and never will that we carry the sin of the world!

## The Mystery of Our Cross Carrying _____

An important point of contact becomes apparent in the way the invitation Jesus gives is reported in just the first three gospels. The issue of our cross is not raised by John; the first three evangelists do speak of this, and these are also the three which mention Simon. It would seem that we need to keep in mind the link between the two—our cross and Simon's. It is not that we are invited to take Simon's place; instead it suggests, along the same lines we have discovered in Mark, that when we take up our cross we ought to be very attentive, extremely attentive even, to the fact that behind us too there is a Simon, carrying our cross with us. He is not in our place, but he is with us; and this Simon, entirely unseen and silent, is none other than God, our Father. We will never see him, as one does not see a person at one's back, and above all if he is invisible anyway. We may well never hear him, silent as he is, but is it not extraordinary and wonderful to know his presence so full of compassion and of such humility? Are we aware of this? The Father is behind us to carry our cross with us; it is unbelievable!

Why did Jesus never speak of this to his disciples to encourage them, neither at the moment when he invited them to take up their cross nor any time afterwards? Why did he say nothing of this? Simply because it is beyond our belief, incredible! This really overturns the image we have of God! We never get to think that God could be so humble, so loving; it is so far beyond our understanding!

And yet, when Jesus tells us that his Father is also our Father (John 20:17), what does he mean to say if not that, what the Father, in his humble love, does for him, he is well able to do also for us, for us who are also his children, and with the same humble love. His love for each of us is the same!

How wonderful! What humble love this is!

Why then did Jesus not say this, announce it, promise it or even suggest it? Because it is inexpressible, beyond our comprehension; the reality of it is not in the realm of knowledge but only of experience. It is only as we carry our cross that we can discover the reality. We cannot really prepare ourselves for this; we can only open ourselves up in prayer since it is in prayer that we open ourselves to the reality of God. We open up without making any demands, as humbly as possible.

## The Imperceptible Presence

To repeat once more, what we experience remains beyond words, in part because there are no words to describe the unseen and silent presence of the Father, but also because his presence remains in the realm of the imperceptible. With what are we dealing? If it were a Simon, no doubt we could hear the sound behind us of him carrying the cross with us, but the sound of God's footsteps? We might hear the sound of Simon's breathing behind us as he exerts himself, but God's? Sometimes it is given to us to perceive the imperceptible God, not because our spiritual ear is somehow more finely tuned than others, but just by pure grace, as a genuine gift, as it was given one day to Elijah to hear the still small voice of God.

But don't forget, never forget, that even if you perceive nothing of God, he is there. I say this even when our cross brings nothing but suffering and the suffering overwhelms our sensibilities and our perception of reality to the point that we feel nothing other than the suffering, when we are unable to feel the compassion of others and those closest to us; it is suffering so strong that it stupefies our understanding. Even then, reader friend, consider the truth as an act of pure faith that your Father is there, bearing the pain of your cross with you.

"Daily, day by day," Jesus says of our cross. These words take on a new savor, both wonderful and inexpressible, the savor of the reality of the Father's presence. In his humble love, he stays right behind us to carry our cross with us, and this is a reality not just of the last day or the first day, but of every day. This is a wonder that draws from us thanksgiving, even while the cross is weighing on our shoulders. No,

Jesus is no sadist when he asks us to take up our cross each day, but rather he intends that each day be one of closeness to God, an overture to the mystery of his humble love.

## Perceiving the Imperceptible

Is the imperceptible presence really imperceptible? In one way it is as imperceptible as the unfelt presence of the Father in the secrecy of our room when we turn to prayer (Matt 6:6). But this is not the whole thing! In reality, when the Father carries our cross with us, the most important thing is not that we feel that he is really there but that we are aware of the effects, the results, the fruit, to know the lightening of the load of the cross on our shoulders. Because of this effect, we can know with joy the presence of the Father; not by the sound of his feet on the ground, but because the cross becomes lighter. It is the case that on occasion we feel him, particularly in prayer, precisely because it is in prayer that we are most open to his presence. To pray without ceasing is to be always open to his presence, as Jesus prayed without ceasing along his way to the cross.

You undoubtedly have had the experience of starting to pray feeling tired, run down, discouraged, crushed, sad, and weighed down by the cross, but leave the place of prayer feeling quite different—rested, renewed, strengthened, lighter, relaxed, peaceful, joyful—and without knowing how the change took place. This change as we pray could surely come only from God. This is the evidence that he has come to lift our burden, our cross—not to rid us of it, but to lighten it. In this way the humble love of the Father becomes a reality to us and we know it by the fruit. This is not knowledge gained from book learning but from the reality of experience, a tangible lived reality. So, we perceive the imperceptible.

This particular type of awareness can also be experienced through the meditation of the word of God in the Scriptures, again not at the level of cerebral knowledge but at the level of lived experience. We can open the Bible, tired, weighed down, discouraged, worn, sad at heart, and feel quite different by the time we close it. We have tasted the imperceptible fruit of his presence.

## Being Simon to Each Other

As we walk the way of the cross it often becomes our turn to be a Simon to a brother or indeed to a stranger, to help them carry their cross. We might act from the goodness of our heart, acting freely, but sometimes we might be under some constraint, obligated by the nature of things, "requisitioned" much as Simon was, so that we are unable to act otherwise, despite ourselves. As humbly as possible, we need to be Simon to our friend, with all the love that we can draw upon from our heart, without seeking any recompense or expectation of thanks—bringing up the rear, not attracting any attention, in the background and silent as was Simon. Then, doubtless, on the last day when we appear before his throne, Christ will say to us, "I was hungry and you gave me to eat; I was thirsty and you gave me to drink; I was a stranger and you took me in; I was naked and you clothed me; I was sick and you visited me; I was in prison and you came to see me . . . I carried my cross and you came to carry it with me" (Matt 25:31–46).

Indeed, if at some moment of your life you realize that standing behind you is a brother or stranger—a Simon come up out of the country requisitioned to help you carry your cross—then, reader friend, invite heaven and earth to join their voices with yours to sing the song of heaven. Truly you will know that through this Simon, and perhaps unbeknown to you, it is the Father, your Father, who in his humble love has come to carry your cross with you.

## Being Requisitioned

Simon was requisitioned; to put it another way, he could not have done other than carry Christ's cross. He couldn't refuse and had no choice; the soldiers had no concern for his rights. That is the meaning of the word "requisition," *angareuō* in the Greek, a word whose Persian origin expresses an unalterable urgency. The word expresses the implacable nature of the law of the Medes and Persians, "which changes not" (Dan 6:12).

So, this was an imposition on Simon. What does this mean for us? Happily we are able at times to choose freely those we help to carry their cross. But it isn't always so, and sometimes we have no choice. There are situations in which we absolutely have to bear the cross of one or another of those near us, of a brother or a stranger; at such times we are requisitioned, despite ourselves, and this may serve to increase our pain. How do we respond to such occasions?

Simon had no choice, his liberty was denied him, scorned by the soldiers; this is true, but it didn't mean that he ceased to be free at heart, either to rebel internally but not show it, or to accept what was demanded of him, and this makes all the difference. It is the same with us; our internal liberty remains even if we are requisitioned.

To carry another's cross without having had the choice and to rebel against it is to close one's heart to the other, remain a stranger to him, to shut out compassion, harden one's heart and not allow any place for love.

To carry another's cross without having had the choice, but still accept it, is to open oneself to the other, join yourself to him, share, carry him in prayer, open yourself to God, walk in love. Through the grace of the Holy Spirit, it is to enter into the inexpressible mystery of the love communion between the Father and the Son.

Where internal revolt is a noisy tumult which chases away internal quiet, internal acceptance opens to the silence and to the desire of entering the indescribable silence of communion between the Father and the Son, in the Holy Spirit.

What is the truth about the internal life of Simon of Cyrene? I don't know, but the fact that his name is recorded seems to indicate that he stayed in contact with the first Christian community and that he was open to the faith, to the Father, to the Son and to the Holy Spirit, and that he had experienced the way of Christ's cross with an open heart, an openness which the Father magnificently honored. The rest belongs in secret to Simon and his bond of love with God.

Blessed Simon, for whom we give thanks.

# CHAPTER 7

# On the Cross

YOU WILL HAVE NOTED the great differences that appear in the four gospels as they relate the hours Jesus spent on the cross. The differences are so great that the gospels even seem to diverge from each other, above all insofar as they concern our main interest, the attitude of God towards Christ, of the Father in relation to the Son. On this subject, though, there is one factor common to the four gospels, which is that God is silent throughout, so much so that the question remains if he is in fact even present.

With regard to the differences, we find in Matthew and Mark that Christ speaks just once on the cross, and addresses God in tones of great pain, with a question which seems to regard any expectation of response as vain: "Why have you forsaken me?" In Luke and John there is nothing so anguished, and no mention is made of this question asked of God; instead, we are given accounts which are much more peaceable and less dramatic.

The difference is underlined by the fact that the only prayer recorded by Matthew and Mark is not addressed to the Father, but simply to, "my God!" whereas the two prayers recorded by Luke are both addressed to the "Father." So far as John is concerned, it is difficult to be definite; disregarding the words spoken to his mother and to the beloved disciple, we don't know if the other words spoken from the cross are prayers or not: "I thirst" (19:28) and "It is finished" (19:30).

This is the situation: on the one hand, Matthew and Mark depicting pain; on the other, Luke, depicting trust, and then John, in doubt between the two.

What attitude should we adopt? It seems to me that it would be duplicitous on my part to choose one gospel and discard the others, just as it would be unfair to treat them all together, blending them and effectively watering them down. What, then, should we do? I propose to start with the most straightforward, which is to say, Luke, where the Son speaks very clearly to the Father; then to turn to Matthew and Mark, where Jesus prays saying, "my God"; and, in order not to overburden this short book, to leave aside John, where it is difficult to know whether the Son speaks to his Father.

We begin, then, with Luke, from the moment Christ is nailed to the cross (23:33) to the time of his death (v. 49).

## "Father, forgive them!"

"Father, forgive them, for they know not what they do!" These are the first words to issue from Jesus' mouth on the cross, and they are a great surprise to us, a great astonishment. Here we have this crucified man, unjustly condemned to death; before him is the crowd that took part in his trial, followed the affair from its inception, and even helped direct the governor's verdict against him. No doubt there are a few friends scattered among them, as well as some women in tears expressing their pity; there are the indifferent soldiers, detailed by the centurion to their work; above all there are his fierce opponents, who wanted his head and had got it. It is composite group gathered around, which we could easily see as a public, an audience which the man on the cross could address while he had strength. Then we see that, without delay, Jesus opens his mouth and begins to speak; what will he say before the whole world? He prays! This is a first surprise; he begins with prayer in a way all could understand. But would this be a pious formula preliminary to haranguing the crowd, a settling of accounts, a demand for vengeance, an attack on the torturers, a denunciation of his adversaries? No, he does nothing but pray. It is nothing but prayer! He prays, and that is all. Then he is quiet. Period!

This prayer must surely grab our attention. It is a prayer limited to one sentence and one alone. Not a psalm which continues until it is all laid out before God, but a single sentence, easy to remember and engrave upon the memory, to which to return in one's heart and carefully consider word by word. This is the best thing to do with it, so let us proceed.

First of all, this solitary sentence in no way centers on Jesus himself, though one would well understand that a man preparing for the ordeal of death, were he to be heard calling upon God to consider him, might focus his attention there. But Jesus doesn't think of himself but of others; he speaks to God about other people, not to complain about them, but to ask for God's mercy on them, not for himself. He prays for all the other people, asking for God's forgiveness of them. Not that some of them be pardoned, but all—friends and enemies alike—including them all in a simple pronoun which neither cuts out nor excludes anyone: "forgive *them*." This is truly wonderful. The simple pronoun is extensive enough that the whole world can feel involved and be beneficiaries of the forgiveness requested, including us too. Jesus' heart is so simply wide open that it can contain the entire world.

## A Public Prayer

This prayer is public. This is already implicit in what we have said, but all the same it needs emphasizing since this is the first time that Jesus prays in front of all the people, and so as to be understood by all. He is known to be a man of prayer, but when he prayed in a crowd it was silently, the content of his prayer being unheard. For the first time, the words of his prayer are heard by all, allowing them all to discover, no doubt to their amazement, his manner of speaking to God; he calls him "Father."

We know that at his baptism, he was praying (3:21), but no one heard the prayer. We know that at the Transfiguration too he was praying (9:29), but the only three disciples present didn't hear what he said. In Gethsemane he had prayed as well, addressing the Father, but the disciples were asleep and didn't hear. On the day he spoke "the Lord's Prayer," only the disciples were there to receive the words (11:2), the same as another moment (10:21) when he addressed his Father. In short, the crowd had never heard him speak out loud in prayer, according, at least, to Luke's gospel. They knew his way of praying scandalized the religious leaders, who accused him of blasphemy, but they had not heard prayer like this, and neither had the religious.

Behold! The crowd hears prayer from the cross! No doubt they were silent, awaiting the consequences. Would lightning fall from heaven on this blasphemer? Would God react, in acquiescence or disapproval? Nothing! Nothing from God! Silence; profound silence!

## Reactions of Those Around

While God didn't react to this prayer, we can see what happened among the crowd, the reactions of those who heard it. What does Luke tell us?

Firstly, Luke reveals the total indifference of the soldiers, upon whom the prayer seems to have no effect. They simply don't listen. Whatever the fellow on the cross might say is nothing to them; what did matter was the man's belongings. How sordid this is; they have no interest in anything other than his clothes, which they part among themselves by lot. How sad! It is really flabbergasting; it was on their behalf too that Jesus had just said, perhaps as he turned his eyes towards them, "Father, forgive them, they know not what they do."

Immediately afterwards, though, Luke tells us something rather wonderful: "the people stood there watching." The word "people," first of all, is a magnificent word and very positive; in the Bible it is a word of great dignity. The people who "stood" are the people who always move the heart of God; not the crowd or the populace, but the people, who God loves, those for whom the angels came to proclaim the glad tidings of the nativity, "[he] will be for all people the cause of great joy" (2:10). It was the people who were at prayer in Jerusalem when the priest Zacharias was offering up the incense (1:10). In short, not the gentiles, not the rag-tag crowd, but "the people" in all their dignity. When God himself pronounces the word "people," he does so with infinite love, even if it is to speak of his own pain; "O, my people, what have I done to you? How have I saddened you," as the prophet Micah reports (6:3).

The people are there, standing, silent, attentive, and expectant. For them, the prayer did not fall to the ground, into the void, on deaf ears, but into their hearts. Luke also adds a fine word which completes the impression, "the people stood watching." Here, the silence stands forth in its beauty, a silence which is attentive, positive, open and even desirous. The people's silence is open full and wide, above all to God, this Father upon whom Jesus has called, and who may perhaps answer. The people, the people beloved of God, listen in silence and watch Jesus, the Beloved Son.

The people "watch." The verb here, *theōreō*, is one which the ancients connected with the words for "God" (*theos*) and "seeing" (*oraō*). This is very apt; the word suggests a look coming from God and turned back towards God, so it is really a very positive, spiritual word, conveying openness to God. We see the people "standing" as if respectfully before God, the heart full of the holy fear one may feel before him. Such is the attitude in which the people watch.

But—pay careful attention here! The people's silence is answered—by the silence of God! What a mystery, what a disturbing mystery. Here, I believe, the people are in full accord with our question: What will God do? What is the meaning of his silence? Does he have some response for Jesus? Is he at least present? You know the litany of questions in the people's hearts that can be told off like the beads of a rosary!

The people stand there, facing Jesus who has just prayed; if God says nothing, will Jesus perhaps speak again and continue his prayer, pray again, insistently before God? He hadn't shouted his prayer from the cross, as though God were distant or not there at all; he had spoken without raising his voice, but loud enough for the people to hear. It is clear that for Jesus, his Father is neither distant nor absent, and that he is listening.

Jesus, however, says nothing more and is quiet. The Father is silent, the Son is silent, and so are the people . . . that is all, but it is very lovely. It is a silence which is no doubt a composite, of disappointment for some, of hope for others . . . but certainly more spiritual than the indifferent soldiers, who are already busy casting dice for the spoils!

This profound silence is brutally interrupted by the religious rulers, who deride Jesus sarcastically (v. 35), intent on vexing and even wounding Jesus' sympathizers. With this tone set, others are encouraged; the soldiers join in with their mocking (v. 36), and to top everything, one of the two other crucified men, one of those alongside Jesus, sets to, bluntly cursing (v. 39). The poor people, suddenly seized by a tempest which swells to drown their contemplation and meditation of Jesus' prayer! As for Jesus, there is no response to any of those who trot out their raillery, mockery and cursing; he holds his peace, his heart, no doubt, turned always towards his Father.

We will turn now to the prayer he spoke, to ponder its contents. We place ourselves among the people and watch with them, our eyes fixed on the cross, attentive to him and to the prayer which has not left his heart or that of the people; the people have not flinched and remain there, opening up to the mystery of the crucified one and his Father.

## The Revelation of the Father

"Father, forgive them, for they don't know what they are doing!" If pardon is asked it must be because of some fault committed, and someone must be responsible; but Jesus is not specific about any particular fault, saying very imprecisely "forgive *them*," so the supposed fault is passed over in silence! It is wonderful to see that Jesus does not denounce anyone, not one person, blames no one and pulls no one down. The people are there, but nevertheless, Jesus gives no invitation to repentance, as had been his practice in Galilee during his ministry; no, he doesn't indicate what the fault or faults committed might be. On the contrary, from the first moment of his prayer, his concern is to reveal the Father to this people who have never heard such a way of praying. This is truly extraordinary; Jesus does not indicate the people's fault, he reveals the fatherhood of God.

"Father." The word drops into the heart of the people, enabling an awareness of God's fatherhood. "No one knows the Father," Jesus had said, "save the Son and him to whom the Son will reveal him" (10:22), and that is what is happening here, on the cross. Jesus reveals the Father as he prays. There is no more beautiful revelation of the Father than in prayer.

At the same time, as he reveals the Father, Jesus shows himself as Son. There the people stand, mute and silent, before the cross and watch; before their eyes is this extraordinary crucified man; the one on the cross is the Son, and more, it is the Son talking to his Father. This is all revealed in the one word, "Father."

"The people watched," Luke writes, without specifying the complement of the verb, simply because it is beyond expression, touching deep into trinitarian intimacy; the Son is there, turned towards the Father in the silence of the Holy Spirit, and this silence envelops the people. We too watch in silence.

## The Father of Mercy

Jesus asks the Father to forgive. In praying like this, Jesus touches the Father in the innermost parts of his compassion and mercy (cf Luke 1:78). Forgiveness is indeed a fruit of mercy, which has its spring deep within; the Father to whom Jesus speaks is a Father of whom one can ask pardon, a merciful Father. For this reason, if the people had a mind to remember, they would recognize in Jesus' prayer their own God, the God who revealed himself to Moses on Sinai in these terms, "I am the Lord, the Lord, a God of tenderness and mercy" (Exod 34:6). This is the God, the God of Abraham, Isaac and Jacob, who Jesus calls "Father." If this God has a heart of mercy, it is because it is the heart of a Father.

Jesus now implores of his Father forgiveness, but in such a way that it seems he had not himself been offended or even concerned as the victim of the fault or sin he passes over in silence. He brings no accusations and makes no endeavor to settle the score with anyone, so this must surely mean that he has himself already forgiven. This perhaps is why Jesus does not now call for repentance; the Jesus who has already forgiven is full of mercy, and in this we might say the Son resembles his Father. Here he is, asking pardon for others, which is to say, both for and in the place of others, for and in the place of those at fault, the guilty ones, and at a time when no one else asks or even feels the need to ask God's forgiveness. It is an amazing thing to find all this in the prayer of a condemned man; he is there before the eyes of the watching people, and before our eyes too as we also watch from among the people.

## The Unstated Fault

As we go further into this extraordinary prayer we find that it remains a mystery on one point at least—knowing what the supposed fault was, the fault implicit in the prayer. Jesus speaks of it as present, not as something past; it is not "forgive them for what they have done" but "what they are doing." It is a prayer factually of that moment, grounded in the present reality; "forgive them for what they are doing right now!" What is this fault which is being enacted, of which the people are witnesses and perhaps even participants? There is good reason to stop and think about this in order to understand a little better; the reason is not curiosity but the desire to dig into the truth of where we are, here and now, in God's sight.

"They don't know what they are doing." Jesus' prayer is stated in such a way as to show that God and Jesus do know. They know without stating or revealing it; they speak covertly, and are united about something we don't know. The prayer thus reveals the fact of the intimacy between the Father and the Son, but it doesn't actually help us penetrate any deeper into its nature; we ponder the Father and the Son in the secret they share, and are bound to respect this. What we also find is that from the secret of this hidden fault will flow forgiveness, which will be poured out upon us. We know we have faults, but we know above all that forgiveness is asked, and that we will no longer be in the place of wrong doers but of those who are forgiven by the Father and by the Son. What wonderful light, which washes away the unknown fault, not because the blame cannot be pinned down, but because of God's forgiveness. What a wonder; the beauty of God is his forgiveness, which makes us forgiven people. It is for this that Jesus prepares us as he prays on the cross, aloud for the people to hear, allowing us to know the request he makes of God on our behalf. What a wonder and what a mystery.

## Modest Compassion

Standing in silence, the people await the requested pardon. They wait with Jesus, who also waits in silence; we await from the Father what

Jesus has asked for us. It is very remarkable: on one hand Jesus is with us, waiting with us; on the other he is communing with the Father over the secret of our fault. There could be no finer intermediary between God and ourselves than Jesus; he has no need to tell us our wrongs; we can trust him. It is enough for us that he carries us in prayer, ready to receive God's pardon. This is so lovely for us!

At this moment we are being carried by the Son's prayer, a prayer which is full of compassion for us; he sympathizes with us because we bear within ourselves the wrong which makes us sinners; he sympathizes and sensitively declines to expose us or make us ashamed. This is wonderful delicacy on the part of Christ, who is full both of compassion and mercy towards us. The compassionate one asks forgiveness for us for a fault which he sensitively hides and, in his mercy, has already pardoned. There is truly matter here to bring us to our knees before him on his cross.

We have not yet spoken of the second thief, the one who did not curse. I believe that it is in the silence that this thief opens his heart to all this, to the mercy, to the compassion and the sensitivity of Jesus; he too has heard the prayer and has perfectly understood the material from which it is fashioned; this is why he says with great simplicity, "Jesus, remember me, when you come into your kingdom!"[1]

"They don't know," says Jesus, speaking about you an me! Jesus also sympathizes with our limited understanding. We are indeed ignorant! We don't know what it is we are doing, unsuspecting that it might even be of the most serious nature; our understanding is so poor, so lacking. God surely knows because he knows everything and nothing is hidden from him; this should suffice for us and satisfy our poor and cramped understanding; we need not ask for anything more but, instead, humbly accept our failure to understand. God knows, even when he is silent as to our faults; and he grants just what Jesus asks—that his forgiveness be revealed but not our failings. Jesus also knows, much

---

1. A chapter in the author's book *From Darkness to Light* follows in detail the process of the "good" thief's conversion. (Trans.)

better than us; we know nothing, but he doesn't mock us for this like the mockers in the crowd; he doesn't deride, he sympathizes. Let us bless him for so forgiving us in his prayer filled with compassion and mercy! Let us bless the Son who resembles his Father in his measureless compassion and mercy!

## The Inexpressible Nature of our Fault

We could, reader friend, be content with this and, like the people in their silence and like Christ who also is silent, await the Father's forgiveness; but perhaps it would be good to go a little further into the mystery of our fault, our wrongdoing, into this thing which is hidden from us, neither unveiled nor denounced by either the Father or the Son. As we go on, it is not to satisfy our curiosity, but so that our thanksgiving may overflow with understanding as we receive the Father's forgiveness; and that we may know the depths of the forgiveness as we come better to know the depths of our fault.

What then is this fault? Jesus says nothing; he doesn't say what is really going on. He says nothing, in part for sure out of his delicate regard for us, but also because there are no words to convey it. Meanwhile, just one word, even if only some approximation, would suffice to set us on the right track; if there was just one word in his brief prayer, something like, "pardon this fault, this sin, this infamy, this abomination"; there is no lack of words which would fix us somewhere on the scale and give some exact value to our sinfulness! Or again, "forgive them for their actions which are irremediable, irrecoverable, unthinkable, indescribable, unpardonable . . ." Would it be, "Father, you who alone can forgive, forgive them this which is unforgivable"? If it were that, I could better understand Jesus' silence as well as that of the Father. Father, is this the case?

I believe that Luke very delicately sets us on the way, which is why I persist with the topic. In effect, I think he opens the way through his choice of words, and then leads us, step by step, gently and silently, to where there are no more words; in fact, there are no words to say what really takes places at Golgotha.

Here is the first step Luke has us take on the way to understanding: when he tells us of Jesus' prayer, he has just written a verse whose final words are, "they crucified him" (v. 33). That is the present reality. The words of Luke's gospel are so organized as to show that this is what Jesus is referring to in his prayer, and when he uses the verb "to do" in the present tense, he's referring to them putting him on the cross; "they don't know what they are doing, crucifying me!" To crucify the Son of God . . . to cause the death of the one most highly honored by God on the most degrading instrument of torture! There truly are no words to express the enormity of this! What word could describe something infinitely worse than infamy? It is indeed unspeakable and unnameable. Nevertheless, reader friend, unspeakable as it is, it is no less true that, for Jesus, what is unspeakable and unnameable is a matter for God's forgiveness! It is pure wonder that it should be so.

I think we can now go further into this; it will not bring condemnation but the conviction that, for us too, this is a matter for God's forgiveness. As we progress, it will be to better receive forgiveness and enable us to give thanks, even if our thanksgiving fails of words and finds itself needing to go beyond anything we can express!

## Back to the Parable of the Vinedressers

At Golgotha, Jesus says nothing of our fault at the moment it is enacted, when it is too painful to speak of—but had he perhaps spoken of it before the cross, while not yet in the fullness of suffering? Did he speak in this way? Well, I believe the answer to be yes, in particular, in the parable of the vinedressers. So if we are to go further, our hearts now humbled and repentant, we need to return to the parable, with its source in Luke, to rediscover how Jesus announced the cross—his death—for it is indeed his death which is now in view. We will go back to the parable, noting how Luke refers back to it.

Mark and Matthew told us that the parable was addressed to the rulers of the people. Luke, however, tells us expressly that Jesus addressed it to "the people"! (20:9) It is extraordinary that the parable was addressed to the very people who are now watching Jesus on the cross; no doubt the people would still have the parable in mind, unforgettable as it was. We will take up the parable, picturing ourselves in the midst of the people watching him there.

Luke noted that the parable itself finishes on a note of great forcefulness, even overwhelming violence; "they murdered him" (v. 15). Jesus had the courage to say this as he told the parable, a few days before the cross, when it was not yet a present reality to him. There are things Jesus could say before the cross which he would never get to say once he was on the cross; there is great difference between announcing something before it happens and when in the middle of it.

As he spoke the parable he could say, "they murdered him," but now that he is on the cross he can't bring himself to say, "Forgive them for murdering me!" Such words desert him, quite simply because he no longer has the heart or taste for them. It would be too hard!

## The Father's Grief

But this, as it seems to me, is not all. In praying as he does from the cross, it is his Father he is addressing, not the people as had been the case when he told the parable; this means still more that, addressing the one whose infinite love is infinitely grieved, he lacks resolve to speak of the present reality; could he really say, "forgive them for murdering your Son before your very eyes"? Surely that is truly impossible, so he is content to say without any addition, "Father, forgive them, they know not what they do!"

On the day he told the parable, as a little investigation will confirm, immediately after he said, "they murdered him," Jesus changed the subject; even then he turned away from saying exactly what would follow. What then does he say after using the term "murder"? He poses the question, "what will the owner of the vineyard do?" We note the choice of words Jesus makes; he speaks of the "owner of the vineyard," the "vinedressers," "the vineyard," not "the father" or "the son." Given the story, he could surely have stated the question more brutally— "what will the father do when he comes and discovers his son dead?" Instead, he glosses over this question and turns to another; he changes the point of reference, displacing the question away from the son and onto the vineyard. Why? Because the son in question is himself. If, as appears to be the case, Jesus had no taste to speak of his own death when it was still only on the horizon, what would he now say when it is so close? Clearly, with what is taking place on the cross, Jesus could no more than suggest it: "Father, they know not what they do."[2]

## The Sensitivity of the Son

In the parable as Luke reports it, we hear from the mouth of the father the expression "my well-beloved son" (v. 13), an expression which is not reported in the other gospels. It is peculiar, then, to Luke to have put this phrase in the father's mouth, and this gives the words particular emotional resonance. It is also equally peculiar to Luke to have underlined in a very strong way the link with the baptism (3:22) and the transfiguration (9:35), where the same words are found in the mouth of the Father. Luke in this way underscores the way the one who says "my well-beloved son" could only be the Father, and this agrees perfectly with Jesus' experience; for him these words are surely unforgettable, doubtless to the point where he could not pronounce them without

2. In the KJV translation the verbal form "what they do" rather than "are doing" displaces their action even more and makes it still more general. (Trans.)

great emotion. This would have been true as he told the parable; how could he now, on the cross, refer to this expression so dear to him? What would he say? Nothing! He certainly can't very well say, "They are murdering your Well-Beloved Son!" That must be impossible! On the contrary, it is amazing that he manages to say "Father." It is as wonderful as it is overwhelming! He manages to speak the word out loud to the whole world, in the presence of the indifferent soldiers and the mocking rulers, but also in the presence of the people, the people who had heard the parable and now maintain a complete silence. It is in the presence of the well-beloved people that Jesus manages to say, "Father, forgive them, for they know not what they do!" After saying this, one can well understand why he says nothing more and remains silent for hours; he has said everything, and there is nothing to add. In one sentence he has expressed his love for his Father, his love for the people, his compassion and his mercy towards all those around him who understand nothing of the depths of his heart or the heart of his Father. Still more, in this brief prayer, Jesus has let the extent be seen of the thirst he has to see us all forgiven; his thirst is immense, so great that we can now readily understand this other word spoken from the cross as reported by John, "I thirst" (19:28). Jesus' thirst on the cross is also the immense thirst he has to see us forgiven; there is so much love in this thirst he has for us.

## The Unspeakable Word

Finally, the word chosen in the parable to say "they murdered him" is not without meaning. It is not the word "murder" from the ten commandments (Exod 20:13; Deut 5:17), which would indicate that the wrongdoers had broken God's law and that their sin was against the law; rather, the word chosen by Jesus shows that this particular death does not touch the law but the Father. By killing the son, the tenants are making an attempt not against the law but against God. It is not so much a sin as a wounding, which takes the reality to a different level. In the end, I believe that this is the word Jesus finds so hard to say; perhaps it is saying the following that he can't manage—"Father, forgive them, because they know not the grief they are causing you!"

Jesus is silent and the Father, too. It seems to me that God's silence thus becomes clear; it is the silence of a Father grieved to his core.

A wound? The word is perhaps accurate, but this doesn't make it other than very understated and inadequate. In fact it's a million miles from reality; we will only really know the depth of what this word means to God when we can measure the depth of the heart we have grieved; which is bottomless! This is why Jesus does so well, once more, to leave the word unspoken and then be silent after he has prayed.

If the Father, in his sorrow, were to try to speak to his people, he too would be unable to find the words, not even to repeat what he had spoken long before in Micah's time—"O my people, what have I done to you; in what way have I harmed you?" It is so as not to hear the pain of his Father that Jesus takes the initiative and says with infinite tenderness, "Father, forgive them, they know not what they do!"

## "Father, forgive us, for we know not what we do" ⸻

Before proceeding any further, reader friend, the text invites us to pause; Luke invites us to take our place among the people watching in silence at the foot of the cross. I believe that the Crucified One invites us, by the prayer he speaks, to identify ourselves in this way. The Father invites us into his grieved silence, and the Holy Spirit impels us to speak Christ's prayer in all simplicity from the depths of our soul, looking deep within and confessing our crushed and broken hearts: "Father, forgive us, we know not what we do!"

Certainly there are the indifferent soldiers, and so many others like them, who will care nothing for our prayer, but this is of little importance; Christ includes them as well as us in his prayer, and asks for them, as for us, the Father's forgiveness.

Certainly there are the rulers who mock and others who curse, and who continue to mock or to curse while we pray, but this too is of little importance; Christ includes all of them as well as us in his prayer, and asks for them, as for us, the Father's forgiveness.

We should pause a little in the midst of the watching people; we should pause at least once in our lives; perhaps more often, every Good Friday maybe, or maybe every Friday, or each time we pass a cross, or maybe each day at the hour he was crucified, whether for a moment or a while, as we are inclined, but we should do this. We should do so with all the love we have in our hearts for the Christ who is crucified before our eyes, and for love of the Father who is also there, grieved and silent.

The intent of the prayer is not to break us but to carry us; it carries us with the strength of the compassion and mercy of Christ, with the trust he has in his Father, the infinite trust that we will be forgiven.

Let us indeed pause a while, our hearts bruised and crushed, in bitter tears of repentance and the sweet tears of knowing that Christ believes that the Father will forgive us.

> Father, forgive us, for we know not what we do!
> We know not how we crucify your Son again, today;
> how we crucify him in the person of the least of our brothers,
> the least of them, whom we deny, whom we betray,
> whom we condemn, whom we slap, whom we ridicule . . .
> Father, forgive us,
> because each time we mistreat the least of our brothers,
> it is your Well-Beloved Son we are mistreating . . .
> Father, in your grace, please receive Christ's prayer, prayed for
> us at Golgotha.

The Father is there, silent and bruised, almost as though a mendicant at the door of our heart, not pushing in but thirsting for us, his children, thirsting for our prayer, thirsting to answer it and forgive us. Like the father of the prodigal, he waits and watches in silence to see if one day he will espy us walking towards him, repentant (see Luke 15:20).

Reader friend, we know what he will do when he sees us turning back to him; we know that he will be so moved in the depths of his being that he will run to meet us and fall on our neck as he takes us in his arms. If we begin to pray to him in this way, perhaps he will interrupt before we finish.

So, in his arms, in Christ, we can rest in deep silence—our heart full of the sweet tears of knowing ourselves truly forgiven.

Before going further, reader friend, let us know that we have stopped and stood at the foot of the cross and said in all simplicity among the watching people:

"Father, forgive us, we know not what we do."

## The Great Day of Forgiveness

"They know not what they do!" Something else that needs to be said about the prayer of Christ is the way it locates us in the atmosphere of the Day of Atonement (Yom Kippur), the great festival of forgiveness. It pushes us in this direction because this festival is the only one in which God is particularly asked to forgive unconscious faults or those committed in ignorance (see Lev 16). All other faults, those which are known, could be confessed and forgiven at any time of the year, but how are we to confess faults we don't know and that are known only to God? The Day of Atonement exists precisely so that God's forgiveness can be sought for these faults. What was Jesus doing on the cross if not asking pardon for what is unknown to anyone except himself and the Father? "Father, forgive them, they know not what they do." This prayer is written into the heart of the Day of Atonement.

Certain details in Luke's account agree entirely with this meaning, and it seems a good idea to draw to attention to these now.

The setting of the Day of Atonement is stated just prior to the crucifixion in the meeting of Jesus with the daughters of Jerusalem along the way to Golgotha. This is mentioned only by Luke; the others gospels say nothing, but Luke tells us that the women weep, beating their breasts as a sign of compassion for the condemned man. What is Jesus' reaction? He tells them to change their tears of compassion into tears of repentance, saying, "Don't weep for me, but weep for yourselves and for your children" (23:28). To invite the women to repentance is to introduce the Day of Atonement.

After Christ's death, Luke tells us—and again he is alone in doing so—that the crowd split up and dispersed, "beating their breasts." This again evokes and puts us into the setting of Atonement. At the end of the day of Atonement, once the ceremonies had been completed, there remained a great question: had the forgiveness requested been granted by God? At the end of the day, vigilance was required of everyone to discern the signs given by God to indicate that his pardon had indeed been given. At Golgotha, as the crowd disperse they are seeking such signs from God. To beat the breast is to repent; it is to wait for forgiveness. This attitude of the crowd shows that, so far as they are concerned, there has been nothing to reveal God's forgiveness. Christ has asked pardon of the Father for all, but has the Father responded to his request?

In short, following Luke's gospel, it seems clear to me: the people who stand and watch are the people of the Day of Atonement awaiting from God the forgiveness requested by Christ.

The points of contact between the Day of Atonement and the cross are also emphasized in the letter to the Hebrews, which develops the theme at length; it invites the conclusion that from thenceforth Good Friday was to be considered as the real day of forgiveness. It is this letter, moreover, that leads me to consider the prayer from the cross as belonging to this festival.

## The Points of Difference

While the points of contact with the Day of Atonement are real, there are also points of difference which in no way negate this reading but do emphasize the extent to which the festival has been modified, renewed and transformed in a definitive way. We won't look at anything other than what Luke says so as to meditate in a focused way.

The main event of Yom Kippur took place in the most secluded area of the Temple, in the Holy of Holies, the most holy place in all Israel, the holiest and purest place. Jesus' prayer is spoken in "the place of the skull" (23:33), so called, as indeed it may well have been, because it was a cemetery; at the very least it was a place of torture, unclean by any standard, because it was the place those condemned to death were executed. There is nowhere more impure than a place for dead bodies. This is a major break with the liturgy, and perhaps explains God's silence; is God likely to accept such a prayer, such a request for pardon spoken in such a sordid place?

To celebrate Yom Kippur, the high priest alone was empowered to enter the Holy of Holies, and was bound to wear particular vestments, as described in detail in the chapter of Leviticus devoted to the festival (16:4); the intent was that no-one appear before God improperly clothed and offend him. Here, on the cross Jesus is basically naked. Is God likely to accept his prayer?

When the high priest entered to ask pardon, he began by asking pardon for his own self and for his family (16:6), with the intent that he not lose his identity with the people. But here Jesus fails to identify in this way, not saying "forgive us," but "forgive them." Wouldn't it make him more of a sinner than any other to pray as he does? Either this is proud blasphemy, or he is unique among men in not being marked by sin. If he is proud to such a degree, will God listen to such a prayer?

Other questions follow: where is the sacrifice offered for the sins of the people. Where also is the scapegoat to carry away the sins of the people? I will leave aside these last questions, leaving you to read to this purpose the letter to the Hebrews; it can be read to great profit.

What strikes me still more in Luke's account is that the prayer spoken by Jesus differs astonishingly from that of the high priest addressed to the Lord in the secret of the sanctuary. In fact, Aaron never called God his Father! He never dared address God in this way; the high priest was no more than a man. Was this fellow, then, greater than Aaron, greater than the high priest? Could he be the Son of God, addressing himself to his Father? Either he is blaspheming outrageously, and his prayer will add grief upon grief to God's heart, or, if he is right, and his prayer is no grief, then it must be a balm to the grief. The people watching the crucifixion could well ask themselves who this man was who could call God his Father in this way and could say, as if to comfort him, "Father, forgive them, for they know not what they do."

## A First Response from the Father

The people await the pardon of God, the Father's answer to the Son's prayer. Jesus is also waiting . . . The silence is intense; the Son is silent, the people are silent, and the Father's silence joins the silence of them all. The people "watch," knowing that God's response would doubtless be some visible sign rather than audible speech; the people are silent, the better to watch.

Before indicating the signs of pardon that all the people could have seen at Golgotha, I wish to draw attention to a sign that Christ alone would have noticed, a silent action of his Father.

In the silence, something extraordinary takes place—something imperceptible to our ears and which escapes the attention of everyone, and of which no one is a witness save Jesus, something which tells us, more than anything, of the Father's forgiveness. Jesus does perceive it and he gently makes it known to one of his two closest "neighbors," crucified with him. I don't know whether many heard what Jesus said to the thief, but he said it, and perhaps some among the people heard it as they stood at the foot of the cross, watching.

Not everyone heard or understood what Jesus said to the thief, since, after Christ's death, the people went their separate ways beating their breasts in real pain, as if God's forgiveness had escaped them or had been refused. Blessed Luke to have reported these words of the man on the cross, concerning us too as they do.

What did Jesus say which this man heard and understood? The thief heard because he was ready to hear; his heart was open to such words, open with great trust, immense hope; I would even say, with great affection. He calls him simply by name, as an intimate, even though he considers him to be a king! "Jesus"—this simple vocative is not found in anyone else's mouth anywhere else in the gospels! "Jesus," the thief says without mockery, but with a trust which is full of affection: "Jesus, remember me when you come into your kingdom!" (23:42). "When you come"; this use of the future by the thief speaks of his immense trust, even when death has already come knocking at his door to accomplish its task!

The thief, ready to hear anything Jesus might say, this thief hears something unprecedented, crazy, unthinkable! Jesus says to him, "Today you will be with me in paradise" (v. 43). "Today in paradise!" How could Jesus say such a thing, such an enormity, when death is knocking at his door too, ready to do what death does? It is indeed an enormity to the ears of some, but it is an unprecedented revelation to the ears of others, beginning with the thief.

If Jesus was able to say such a thing, if he was able at such a moment to speak of paradise, it seems to me that it is simply because he had seen what no one else had seen; he had seen the gateway to paradise open, ready to receive them! That must be it! The gate had been closed since the beginning, since the ancestral fault, the fault common to all, since man had fallen into pride and had done the unforgiveable, listening to the serpent rather than God. Since that day the gate to paradise had been shut by a grieved God, shut up by God's sorrow. Never since that day had the gate been opened, because God had never yet been able to pardon such a cause of grief, so deep. But here today, Jesus had prayed from the cross without the slightest trace of pride, with a humility of the greatest beauty, and with an infinite tenderness which fell as a balm on God's grief, consoling his wounded heart. In this extreme tenderness, he had humbly said, "Father, forgive them, they know not what they do!" These words had touched the Father to the depths of his being; he had received with inexpressible joy his Son's prayer, and in this joy, without saying anything, had silently opened the door to paradise. He had opened it as the prodigal's father had opened the door of his heart to welcome him home. Ah! The silence of the God who opens the door to paradise—this is the silence of the Father during the crucifixion!

The Son had seen the Father open the door, and the words he addressed to the thief contained the forgiveness of God, given to all no doubt—not just to the thief, but to all—since it is for all that the Son had asked pardon. The door would surely not swing shut again behind the thief! It is forever open to all, to all who freely, humbly, with wonderment, receive with confidence the words spoken by Christ to the thief; "I tell you, today you will be with me in paradise!" This "today" is the today of the Day of Atonement.

## The Father's Other Responses

Now, reader friend, we must further pursue our reading of Luke's gospel, at the very least to verify that the "today" of the cross is indeed the great day, the day of forgiveness. Jesus had perceived God's pardon and had announced it to the thief; but is he the only one to have perceived it? Were there other signs given by God, which the people could notice, signs which would make it evident that the prayer of the one on the cross had been received, and that the day is indeed the day of Atonement?

As you know, one peculiarity of the Holy of Holies is that it was entirely dark. This place had no window, no aperture to the exterior. Solomon had constructed it in response to the desire God himself had expressed. Thus, Solomon specifies, "The Lord has desired to dwell in the darkness" (1 Kgs 8:12). This is indeed God's desire, as the psalmist also confirms; "The Lord has made the darkness his refuge" (18:12). Such is the Holy of Holies, a place full of darkness, for God to dwell there.

When Jesus pronounced his prayer for general forgiveness from the impure site of Golgotha, God had shown his approval, responding in a way as surprising as wonderful. He had stretched the darkness of the sanctuary over Golgotha; not only over Golgotha but even over the whole earth! "There was darkness over the whole earth," Luke tells us. In stretching the darkness of the sanctuary over Golgotha, God was purifying this impure place, sanctifying it; the whole earth was purified in this way, sanctified by the sanctifying darkness of the Holy of Holies! Thus the whole earth has become the Holy of Holies! All this in silence; after first of all opening the doorway to paradise in silence, the Father has followed by spreading darkness over the whole earth to make it the Holy of Holies. This is a marvel that, now, all the people could ponder.

At the same time, this holy darkness comes to cover the nakedness of the Crucified, fulfilling the office of clothing of a sort! What kindness on the Father's part to thus veil his Son's nakedness, dressing him with darkness. What tenderness it was too to dress in this way a body so bruised, so pierced and scratched to the quick by the whippings, thorns and the nails . . . the lightest tissue placed on flesh so bruised would quicken the pain. Now the kind darkness gently veils the Crucified One and covers him with the balm of the Father's tenderness.

With this, "the sun disappeared," Luke tells us. The sun, humbly, hides itself; it disappears so as not to shed its light on the new Holy of Holies; it withdraws its light because now another light shines in the Holy of Holies, a light more beautiful than its own; another light shines, that which pours from the one on the cross and enables all to contemplate him as he shines brighter than the sun. Already, to anticipate the end of time, "the holy city has no more need of the sun," as Revelation tells us (21:23), "because the lamb is in it . . ."

Finally, as a crowning event, we know that the only opening to act as an entrance way into the Holy of Holies was bounded by a veil, and the high priest alone could pass through this on the Day of Atonement. On the day of the crucifixion this veil was ripped apart. We do well to say "was ripped" and not "ripped" because it didn't rip on its own as, unhappily, some of our translations would have us think, substituting an active for the passive verb. The veil was ripped by he alone who could do so, by God himself. By doing this, I believe God wished to demonstrate that it was no longer necessary to delimit the Holy of Holies, separating it from the rest of the earth, since the whole earth was the Holy of Holies.

Further yet, I believe that by this action God wished to make it clear that the veil no longer had a reason to exist and that it would no longer be necessary to repeat each year the liturgy of atonement, simply because God's forgiveness had been for ever accorded "once for all," in response to him who asked it "once for all" (Heb 7:27; 9:12). If we still hesitate over the eternal value of what is expressed on the present occasion of Jesus' prayer, then the Father himself, by ripping the veil, shows that what was an occasional event is also an eternal reality for him.

## In the Silence of the Sanctuary

The Holy of Holies has one further particularity: it was a place of silence. Two cherubim alone were to be found there, immersed in an eternal and infinite silence, honoring the silence of God as they offered to God their unceasing adoration, always in silence. Such was the Holy of Holies every day of the year, as if in preparation for that one day, the day of Atonement, when the high priest could enter in silence and pronounce the only name which could be pronounced, the most holy Name of God, never spoken aloud other than there in the most holy place. Such was the Holy of Holies, a jewel-case in which the Name could be deposited, as if into the heart of God.

On this day, as the darkness covered the earth, the silence of the sanctuary also covered the earth from the sixth until the ninth hour. During these three hours, nothing more is heard in the land; the people are silent, enveloped in a silence now become holy, since the earth is become the Holy of Holies. The gospel account is quite startling on this point. The mockery stopped, as did the raillery and cursing. The thief had said all he had to say. Nobody else speaks on this earth turned sanctuary. The entire cosmos waits for the Name to be spoken, the Name which one alone is qualified to speak. He alone is worthy to pronounce this holy Name; he alone is capable of speaking it with the humble love which is appropriate; he alone is perfectly possessed of that humble love in a measure equal to the humble love of God.

Then, in this silence which has lasted three hours, Jesus opens his mouth to make known the Name which no other before him had known to speak in this way; he pronounces it "in a loud voice," Luke tells us, a voice loud enough for the whole cosmos to hear and bow before. He pronounces it with the humble love which is beyond all other humility and love; he pronounces it with infinite tenderness.

From up on the cross, Jesus says, "Father . . ."

He alone could say this name because he alone is truly the Son in the way the Father is truly the Father.

"Father, into your hands I commit my spirit."

The Father welcomes with infinite tenderness the Son, who hands himself over in infinite trust.

## "Father, into your hands I commit my spirit" ⸻

Between the sixth and the ninth hours, between the disappearance of the sun and the tearing of the veil, nothing further took place—or rather, Luke, as he looks into the inexpressible mystery of God, says nothing more. He mentions no other person, points to nothing else he might have described; he puts a period, as it were, in the middle of the line and lifts his pen. He too was gripped by the silence; he ponders the Crucified One, who shines brighter than the sun. He watches as the crowd watches, as a few women towards the back also watch, as the thief watches, and as the centurion opens his heart to watch. In this deep contemplative silence, Jesus, at the center, prays.

This is for three whole hours! And the Father is silent . . . !

Christ prays at the moment of his death, and here we discover in his final prayer that he is also deeply informed by the prayer of his people; lodged deep in him are the psalms, which he carries in himself and which have fashioned him since his early childhood. So it is that his altogether final prayer, spoken as he dies on the cross, is a verse from the psalm; "into thy hands, I commit my spirit" (31:6).

Indeed, this prayer is taken from a psalm, indicating again Christ's extreme humility. Jesus does not die speaking a prayer of his own composition—a prayer which would be his own, which would demonstrate the great spiritual height he has reached, giving us a prayer which is sublime and beyond the common. No, he dies a death so humble that on his lips are words from the tradition of his people, a prayer he received from them! Christ is humble, so attached to his people that he still allows himself to be led by them in his prayer. He received the psalms from his people, and he now returns them at the moment of his death, as if saying to those of his own who are there at the foot of the cross, watching, "O, my people, you have given me everything in giving me the psalms; I now give them back to you."

However, as he returns the psalms to the people beholding the cross, Jesus adds a small note to be theirs from that day forward. Jesus adds, in fact, one little word, but of infinite richness; it is the very first word of his prayer, "Father." "O, my people, you have taught me to pray with the psalms; from this day pray them addressing them with me to my Father, to my Father who is also your Father. You have given me everything by giving me these psalms, and I give you everything by giving you my Father." The fact is that this psalm no more than any other says "Father" to God; but starting with Christ, that is the way our praying of the psalms is now to be done, opening our hearts to the Father, just as Christ taught us from the cross.

"O, my people," he adds, "like me you have received the psalms from David and the Holy Spirit; I give them back to you so that from now on you can affirm them with me, with the Father and with the Holy Spirit."

Indeed, this is how we pray them today.[3]

## The Torn Garment

"Between the sixth and the ninth hour." This is the only time anywhere in the gospel that Luke records the passing hours, the flow of time. It shows us that these hours well and truly pertain to our history. It is very much an incarnated moment, with no escape or evasion of time. It is a period that the Father himself comes to share with us, astonishingly present, so present indeed to us and to his Son that he receives full into his heart the reality of the Crucified One's death. With the death of the Son, the Father now knows the bottomless pain of every father who sees his child die. This pain is so great as to make him know to the depths what grief can be, the grief of a father. Now the Father, in grief, without hiding his feelings, performs an action of intense sorrow: he tears his garment. This is how it sounds in the ears of all, in the measureless silence of Golgotha, "the veil of the temple was ripped in two." In this tearing, ripping, we hear the tearing of the Father's heart.

3. See the author's book *Praying the Psalms*. (Trans.)

It is a sorrow so profound that it is beyond words; a mute, wordless ripping beyond any other.

It is a sorrow so great and so fills the heart of the people that soon after, Luke tells us, they went away, beating their breasts (23:48).

This is assuredly a humble Father who abases himself into the midst of our actuality to the point of profoundly experiencing sorrow. But he is also a humble Father in that he goes so far as to do what was forbidden to the chief priest (Lev 21:10, "he shall not rend his garment"). This was forbidden exactly because the chief priest alone was able to enter the Holy of Holies, and because this act of grief carries with it the stench of death. There was no way such a stench should be allowed to pervade a place devoted to incense. The smell of death has no place in the sanctuary of the God of life. Here, God himself, this Father of such humility, makes himself less than the high priest, sharing with all humanity the stench of grief.

Behold this humble Father, who so loves his crucified Son!

The Son has understood the tearing of the veil; he has perceived the pain of his Father. Now in such great compassion towards his Father, he comes in prayer to apply all his tenderness to his torn heart, to comfort him: "Father, into thy hands I commit my spirit."

As he returns his spirit to the Father, he also returns the Comforter.

What humble love of the Son for the Father!

Having said this, he expires . . .

At the time of his baptism, the Holy Spirit humbly descended from the Father to the Son; now, with the Son's last breath, he goes humbly from the Son to the Father.

What an inexpressible communion of love!

# CHAPTER 8

# Joseph of Arimathea

He stretched out his hands on the cross and we have given him death . . .

He stretched out his hands on the cross and he has given us life . . .

For our part, it is a murder, according to the world's logic, which is void of love . . .

For his part, it is an offering, according to God's logic, the very summit of love . . .

He is there, and our eyes are averted; shame covers our faces and brings us to the most bitter of tears:

Lord Jesus Christ, Son of God, have mercy on us, sinners!

He is there, and our eyes never leave him; thanksgiving fills our hearts; we shed the sweetest of tears:

Lord Jesus Christ, Son of God, may you be blessed eternally!

WHO NOW WILL TAKE him down from the cross to place him in the tomb?

The laying of Christ's body in the tomb is related to us in all four gospels; we have a choice, if we wish, to stay with just one as we ponder this scene in the Passion, though we should not neglect the others.

Which of the four would immediately be the most appropriate to help us perceive the attitude and the role of God the Father, and how he experienced this portion of events? First, we find that God's silence in the four gospel accounts is total, so much so that we might once again question if he is even present. Nothing, at a first reading, would enable us to see how the Father saw the burial of the Son.

The previous sign that would indicate the Father's presence is the rending of the temple veil, which, unlike Luke, Matthew and Mark situate not before but immediately after Christ's death. This discreetly but wonderfully reveals the Father's grief at the death of his Son. This overwhelming action, performed wordlessly, is certainly the sign of a grief beyond words, beyond all grief.

After rending his garment, what did the grief-stricken Father do next? How did he manage as his Son was taken down from the cross and laid in the tomb? Nothing is apparent in the gospel accounts, no doubt because the mystery of the Father's grief is too deep for us! Whatever else, we may chase from our hearts any suggestion of an indifferent, unfeeling Father. His grief is there, indicated by the tearing of the veil; it is there, inescapably, and no doubt beyond anything we could say, or beyond anything the four evangelists themselves could say.

We could just stop humbly here and kneel at the threshold of the mystery of God's grief, in repentance and compassion before it. But before we turn away, there is still time to look at everything Christ said to see if there is anything further which can enlighten our thoughts.

In the announcements Jesus makes of his Passion, the mention of his death is each time followed immediately by him speaking of the resurrection. Nowhere does he speak of being laid in a tomb. There is, nevertheless, one place where he does speak of it; this is when he spoke to the woman who poured ointment over his head (Mark 14:3). The indignation at this caused Christ to respond: "She has anointed my body for burial beforehand" (14:8). He frankly speaks of his burial; he reveals the advance participation in it of this woman, but this says nothing that sheds light on the attitude of the Father.

## To the Parable of the Vinedressers Again

Once again it is in the parable of the vinedressers that we find an expression which will wonderfully illuminate things and helps us progress a little into the mystery of the Father's mourning. This light from the parable is found in just one gospel, and this will cause us to focus on this gospel in particular as we incline our ears to its account of the burial.

One expression alone in the parable casts light on the point which occupies us, which is to say that the way in which the Son reveals the Father is with extreme discretion and sensitivity, difficult as it must have been for him to evoke his Father's mourning. This is so true; how distressing it must have been for him to speak of his Father's pain!

As we have seen, this parable is recorded by the first three evangelists alone, which means we can discount John from our investigation. Matthew and Luke, as again we have seen, both finish their accounts with the word "kill" with regard to the son: "they killed him." The word is coupled in their versions with another detail, but following it: "they cast him out of the vineyard and killed him." This captures factually the reality of the Passion, and effectively is the order of things as experienced by Christ, first led out to Golgotha, which is to say out of the city, "cast out" in some sense from the vineyard, before being "killed" on the cross.

## The Humiliation

Mark presents things differently, using the same terms but inverting the order, which considerably changes the sense. Here is his text: "they killed him and cast him out of the vineyard" (12:8). The difference with Matthew and Luke is a large one. In effect, we find here that the son is not taken alive out of the vineyard before being killed, but first of all he is killed, so that when he is thrown out he is already dead. I must ask you to forgive me for being so crude, but it is the son's corpse which is thrown out by the tenants, with the sordid idea that they are disembarrassing themselves of a corpse because it is an encumbrance to the vineyard, of which they now intend to take full possession. Forgive me for evoking this humiliation so crudely where Christ expresses it with such discretion, but the ignominy is really there in these few words, "they killed him and cast him out of the vineyard."

This is the parable as Mark records it and he alone. Is it he who has modified the parable properly conserved by Matthew and Luke? Or is it the reverse, that Matthew and Luke modified what Mark recorded correctly? What in fact was the parable at this point as Jesus spoke it?

It seems to me that Matthew and Luke modified things in order to conform the parable to events as they happened to Jesus, first being led out from the city alive to Golgotha, before being put to death. This harmonization with Jesus' experience would therefore be an adaptation and not the original, at least on this point. I believe, then, that it is Mark who was faithful at this point to the parable as spoken by Jesus. Jesus' concern was not particularly to predict what would happen on the day of his death; rather, he was focused more on the owner of the vineyard than on the son, more attentive to the Father than concerned with himself. It is also true to say that Mark's report fits better with the overall pattern of the parable; it presents the owner as preoccupied with the thought of the tenants' respect for his son—"they will respect my son!" This thought never leaves the father's heart; the parable is surely centered on this question of respect for the son. What, then, happened? How did the tenants behave? Killing the son is a flagrant sign of disrespect, and if we follow Matthew and Luke, the parable stops there, on this lack of respect. Mark, however, goes a step further in this lack of respect. It is already so base to kill the son, but still worse to throw out the body with no care for its burial; this is an insupportable offhandedness and contempt; "they killed him and threw him out of the vineyard." In the end, the tenants did not even bury the body but left it to the crows; there could hardly be a greater humiliation. The tenants go beyond the threshold of disrespect and reach its very heart.

This is what Mark faithfully reports from Jesus' teaching: the height of disrespect where God expected respect. With tremendous delicacy and wonderful sensitivity vis-à-vis his Father, Jesus evokes, in just a few words, through the person of the vineyard owner, the unspeakable pain of the Father.

## What Will the Father Do?

In this way the parable in Mark reaches a peak of disrespect, and this now raises another question: who will be responsible for the son's burial, bearing in mind that the only characters present in the story are the father and the tenants? The tenants are certainly not going to make an effort to see to the interment of the son, not after "throwing" the dead body out. Who then? The remainder of the parable is distressing and leaves in suspense what we can only guess and suppose by using our imaginations; it is the father who will have to bury the son!

This lodges in our spirits. When Jesus continues the parable he says, "what will the owner of the vineyard now do?" and gives the answer to the question himself, continuing, "he will come . . ." One imagines the logical consequence, picturing the father arriving at his vineyard, looking for his son and searching until the moment he finds the body. But we should allow Jesus to continue; what he says next is most surprising. Jesus simply bypasses the all too painful reality to focus not on the dead son, but the fate of the tenants. Evoking the dreadfully pained father discovering the son's body leaves Jesus speechless; he can't bring himself to speak of it. He passes over it in silence, and in the silence drops into our heart this mute and inexpressible scene of a father discovering his dead son. What will he do after rending his garment in his extremity of sorrow? Is he going to bury his well-beloved son alone, performing for him the acts of his infinite respect, infinite tenderness and infinite love? Jesus drops this into our heart with the conviction that we will know, surely, who the son in the parable is, and who the father is who discovers the body, for the burial of which he now finds himself responsible. No word exists to speak the pain of this father; in any case, if the words do exist, they won't be found on Jesus' lips. It is enough for Jesus just to drop this inexpressible scene into our hearts, a scene made still more inexpressible when the father in question is none other than God, his Father. All this is no more than a parable, but it still immerses us in an infinite mystery, to think of God as burying Christ, the Father burying the Son!

## "He will come" . . . "he comes"

Thus prepared by the parable, as reported to us by Mark, we can now turn to the account of Christ being laid in the tomb as found from the pen of the same evangelist (15:42–47). He, more than the others, is bound to be particularly attentive to the role of the Father in this episode of the Passion. We will not ignore the accounts of Matthew, Luke, or even John, but we will now ponder Christ's burial in the way Mark invites us to.

"What will the owner of the vineyard do?" Jesus asked, after speaking of the son's death. As we saw, Jesus continued, "He will come . . ." and, as we confirmed, then immediately switched direction, and changed the subject. This "he will come" is therefore the last important word before the complete silence with regard to the body of the son. Now, here in the narrative of the Passion, after relating the crucifixion and death of Christ, at the moment he turns to the burial, Mark begins his account exactly where he finished the parable. He starts with the verb "come"—"he comes" (v. 42)—which, taking a literary view, is a most beautiful linkage. It is a very nice connection, certainly, but it contains a surprise when we discover the subject of the verb; the one who comes, Mark says, is another well-known unknown—one Joseph of Arimathea.

## The Mysterious Joseph

Who is Joseph? He is unknown to the reader of the gospels, someone who neither Mark nor the other evangelists have named previously to this scene, someone who emerges from a silence into which—since the rest of the New Testament makes no further mention of him—he immediately returns. At first sight, Joseph seems somewhat similar to Simon of Cyrene, both of them coming out of the silence and then returning to it.

Joseph is a native of Arimathea, which is a town unknown in the Old Testament and not mentioned in the remainder of the New Testament. Is it perhaps Ramathaim, Samuel's hometown, as some modern commentators think? It is not obviously so, despite the similarity of the names; Ramathaim is called Armathaim in the Greek of the Septuagint (1 Sam 1:1), which is close but not the same as Arimathea. In short, I believe that Arimathea is a town otherwise unknown in the Scriptures, which for us means that Joseph is to be considered a man emerging from mystery, from secrecy, perhaps even the mystery of God.

Matthew tells us that Joseph was a disciple of Jesus (27:57), to which John is quick to add that he was a disciple "in secret" (19:38), and this helps maintain the aura of mystery around the man.

Here then is a man who emerges from secrecy and dares to go to Pilate to claim the body of Jesus; this outcome implies an exchange of words, but Mark doesn't record any of the conversation, satisfied just to state the substance of the transaction. Subsequently, after leaving Pilate, Joseph is pictured as a man who is completely silent; from the time he is at Golgotha, in contact with Jesus' body, everything Joseph does is conducted in silence, as he takes the body down from the cross until it is laid in the tomb; afterwards, he is shrouded again in secrecy, the silent mystery of God.

## The Silence of Golgotha

Joseph's silence is underscored by the presence of the women who are there throughout, also in total silence (15:47). Before Joseph's arrival, the women were already at Golgotha, standing near the cross (15:40), silent. When he gets there, their silence remains unbroken, which is most surprising. It was the custom under such circumstances that the women would make their cries of mourning heard (Matt 9:23; Jer 9:16; Ezek 32:16); a burial would always be accompanied by the lamentations of the women, who were actually termed "mourning women." There was none of that here, though, for Christ; the women maintained a total silence. Joseph buried Jesus without eliciting anything from them but silence. They were content, Mark tells us, to "watch" (v. 47).

According to Matthew, the natural world responded violently to Jesus' death, with an earthquake and the splitting of rocks (27:51–52). This is not mentioned in Mark, who speaks only of the rending of the veil, not an event of any cosmic order; the Father expresses his grief, but creation itself is silent. Silence reigns on Golgotha. The centurion is alone in speaking briefly immediately after Christ's death (15:39), and these are the last words to be heard. When Joseph arrives, he is greeted by a profound silence; he enters in a silence from which he does not emerge.

There are no angels from heaven as at the Nativity, or as there would be on either Easter morning or at the Ascension; no divine message to be heard. Heaven is as silent as the Father, no doubt to share his grief.

Discreetly, Mark makes Joseph's arrival coincide with the imminent onset of the Sabbath (v. 42), but the Sabbath preparation on Golgotha unfolded without any formalities. According to the tradition, there was a liturgy for the Sabbath, and this was normally entrusted to the women. This would focus our attention upon those who are there, but they intone no song or prayer . . . nothing but silence.

The mention of the Sabbath at the start of the narrative centered on Joseph turns our attention to the fact that, with the Sabbath, we enter into God's rest or silence. One of the characteristics of the Sabbath is precisely that from the beginning of the world—and in contrast to all the other days of the week—this is the day that God ceases to speak (Gen 2:1–3). Joseph arrives at Golgotha in the silence of God. He could not be other than one with the Father's silence, and enters deeply into it as he cares for the Son, takes him down from the cross, wraps him in a linen cloth, lays him in a sepulcher, and then rolls the stone across its entrance.

All is silent on Golgotha, an infinite and deep silence which unites the Father, Joseph, the women, creation, the heavenly host . . . all gathered around the Son, who is thus entrusted to the silence of death.

## One Alone for the Burial

Not only is Joseph silent but he is also quite on his own to accomplish what his heart has undertaken, a task which in truth seems impossible for one man alone. How could this one man alone have taken the crucified body down from the cross? How could he alone wrap him in the linen cloth, and lay him in the tomb on his own? Could he alone roll the stone across, a stone which Mark's phrasing avers to have been "very large" (16:4)? In describing the stone, Mark seems to have deliberately underlined that what Joseph did seems impossible. John (20:1) and Luke (24:2) speak of the stone without going into detail as to its size, while Matthew tells us that it was "large"; Mark overdoes them by far when he says it was "very large." I don't believe that Mark wished to depict Joseph as some kind of superman, but rather he endeavored to convey that there is a mystery which envelops Joseph and is much bigger than him.

With this man on his own, the women "watch" what's going on, just as they had "watched" Jesus on the cross while keeping their distance. No doubt that is where they stayed to watch Joseph as he cared for Christ. They watch without intervening, which is still more surprising; at the very moment when the crucified body is being wrapped in linen, they do nothing to help the lone man in a task which traditionally belonged to women.

The women neither move nor intervene; they seem to be held back by something outside of themselves, perhaps suggestive of mystery. From the time they get to Golgotha, they do nothing but "watch" Christ; this is their role.

"They watch" (*theōreō*): Mark's choice of this particular word is significant. As we have already seen (Luke 23:35), this word is always tied to the mystery of God. In using this form, Mark simply suggests that there is something going on which is beyond what a superficial look would reveal, something of God, which would explain the behavior of the women, who are silent when it would have been quite otherwise were it an ordinary burial.

So, what is happening? What is the mystery watched by the women, the mystery which seems to wrap itself around Joseph?

The mystery appears to me to be that Jesus' burial is undertaken entirely by one man on his own, which seems to be something impossible. When John recounts this scene he seems to have noted this and he departs from Mark, as from Matthew and Luke, in noting Nicodemus alongside Joseph, so that really there is no mystery; Joseph and Nicodemus together took Jesus' body down from the cross, together wrapped him in linen cloth, and together laid him in the tomb (19:40–42). There is nothing in the accomplishment of these tasks impossible for two men.

A burial undertaken by one man does indeed seem impossible; there is no lack of examples to show that more are always needed.

We need dwell on just one, also mentioned by Mark, that of John the Baptist, which is very reasonably described as involving many: "John's disciples came to take his body and place it in a tomb" (6:29).

This seems so obvious that Paul himself sides with what seems possible, speaking of Jesus' burial as being enacted by more than one; "they took him down from the tree and laid him in a tomb" (Acts 13:29). Does Paul base his view on John's account or someone else, in speaking this way? I don't know. With him it must be founded on the evidence that burials are the work of several people.

Why then does Mark accentuate at this point that Joseph was acting alone throughout the unsparing care he gives to Christ? What is the mystery which the women watch and ponder, and means that they never take their eyes off Jesus, all the while at a distance?

## Moses's Burial

If we make a review of all the burials mentioned in the Bible, we find that no one was ever buried by one person alone, with one exception, which concerns the deepest of mysteries. I believe that it is towards this mystery that Mark is leading us, always observing the great discretion with which such a matter should be surrounded.

Throughout the Bible there is just the one burial conducted by a single person—that of Moses, God's friend, his intimate (Exod 33:11). Just before it tells us about this burial, the biblical account first mentions Moses's death, describing it with a simple expression, in itself already enough to surround us with an infinite mystery of love. It tells us that Moses died "from the mouth of the Lord" (Deut 34:5). Translators and commentators of this phrase oscillate between two possibilities: some, thinking that basically it refers to words which come from God's mouth, translate this as, "he died according to the word of the Lord"; others, supposing that something else could issue from God's mouth, say that "he died with a kiss from God." I leave you to choose for yourself, reader friend, but for myself I have to say I am unable to understand this other than a death "with a kiss from God." This seems to line up with the mystery of God's love. Before the infinite mystery of God's love, we prostrate ourselves in silence. This is the direction I am impelled by what we learn of the death of God's friend: wonderment, prostration, and silence.

After speaking like this of Moses's death, the text in Deuteronomy continues with the simple words, "and he buried him" (34:6), and concludes with this brief statement, "and no one knows the place of his burial to this day." This is all, but it is perhaps already too much. To the mystery of Moses's death is added that of his burial. "He buried him," which is to say, "the Lord buried Moses."

"He buried him." This simple phrase so overflows with mystery that I can, once again, only marvel and bow down in silence.

To say that no one knows where his grave is to be found underlines the way Moses's burial had no witness and that everything took place in the fathomless intimacy between God and his friend. The mystery is so great that the biblical text carefully guards against describing the indescribable, or opening our imaginations to the unimaginable. The burial shines only with the inaccessible light of God. God so loves this man who died in his kiss that he takes great care to bury him in the solitude of intimacy. This love is so humble that he doesn't recoil from a task which, according to the Law, even the chief priest was not allowed to perform. In fact, the chief priest was not allowed to participate in any burial, to avoid being defiled by the impurity of a dead body (Lev 21:11). What a humble God, who considers himself less important than the chief priest!

What humble love of God for his friend! A humble love so inexpressible it can only be approached in the silence of adoration.

"He buried him." Faced with such a mystery, all the early translators of this expression found themselves in a huge dilemma; the translations reveal their embarrassment, some of them taking nothing away from the mystery of such a disconcerting God, while others ride over it, no doubt proposing to preserve God's honor. We need to discuss this a little, the better to understand what happened when Christ was laid in the tomb.

Some ancient translators have kept very close to the Hebrew: "he buried him"—as found in the Jonathan Targum, the Onquelos Targum, and the Syriac version; others draw back from the mystery and rub it out, putting the verb in the plural, "they buried him"—as found in the Neophiti Targum, the Samaritan text, the Greek (Septuagint) and the Latin (Vulgate). This plural translation puts men in God's place and does away with the mystery. What a shame, reader friend, that this dissolving of the mystery should be found precisely in the Septuagint and the Vulgate, since the Fathers, both Greek and Latin, knew nothing of this revelation of God which is so revealing of his humble love. What a shame; it would have been so good had they pondered this mystery and helped us meditate it, as they have with other mysteries.

It is just the same with Jesus' burial, where we find a similar disjunction. For Matthew, Mark, and Luke, he was buried by just one person; for John and Paul, he was buried by more than one.

That is how it is with Christ's burial—performed by just one man, just like that of Moses by God after dying in a divine kiss.

## Behind Joseph

When Jesus told the parable of the vinedressers he stopped at the edge of the mystery, after saying the son had been killed and his body cast out of the vineyard without burial. "He will come," he continued, speaking of the father, but leaving open the question of burial. Jesus suggested it without going further. The measureless pain of his Father held him back on the threshold of the inexpressible.

As he now relates Christ's burial, Mark invites us to picture that behind Joseph, it is the Father in his humble love who buries his Son. This is so much beyond expression that he doesn't say it explicitly.

Mark does not say anything about the Father; he only talks about Joseph, but he does this in terms which endow him with an aura of mystery: he comes from an unknown town, accomplishes a superhuman task on his own in a silence replete with reverence and veneration, in the presence of women who only watch, standing at a distance as before a burning bush.

What more can I say without becoming excessive or profaning a mystery? Mark himself does neither; he invites us to stand alongside the women and watch Joseph with them, and, through Joseph standing behind him, the Father, invisible, indescribable, in his unfathomable humble love. Mark retains an admirable sobriety which opens onto mystery and reverence.

Joseph's actions at Golgotha occupy just one verse: "he took him down, wrapped him in a linen cloth, laid him in a tomb hollowed out of the rock and rolled a stone over the entrance to the tomb." We will dwell a little on these words, charged as they are with the full depth of the Father's love for the Son.

First of all, a remark on the complement of the verbs: he took *him* down, wrapped *him* in a linen cloth, laid *him* in a tomb. What Joseph asked of Pilate was "the body of Jesus" (v. 43); however, what Pilate gave him was not the "body" (*sōma*) as requested, but the "corpse" (*ptōma*) of Jesus (v. 45). This change of wording well represents what Jesus meant to the two men. For Pilate this was nothing more than a corpse; for Joseph, it was much more. This "secret disciple," as John terms him, asked for Jesus' body, which seems discreetly to suggest the mystery of the one who passed around the bread, saying, "this is my body" (14:22). The depths of this word may well suggest the Eucharistic mystery; Joseph receives into his hands the body of Christ.

In the passage that refers to taking him down from the cross, wrapping him in linen, and laying him in the tomb, Mark doesn't use the neuter pronouns which would refer to the dead body or corpse of Jesus; instead, we find the masculine pronouns which could only designate Jesus. This light touch is unique to Mark; the other evangelists use the neuter forms and so speak of Jesus' body. By using the masculine Mark focuses attention not on the body but on the person of Jesus, and so on the mystery of his person in the heart of the Father.

"He took him down, wrapped him in a linen cloth, laid him in the tomb." These verbs all describe physical contact and we know the importance in biblical thought of the defilement caused by touching a dead body. But here, things are quite different; beyond questions of purity and impurity, we are concerned with the Father and the Son and their bond of love, the purity of which is so extraordinary that nothing could defile it, not even death.

"He who hangs on a tree is cursed by God," says the Law (Deut 21:22–23). Here is another mystery offered for our contemplation; he who became a curse according to the Law becomes a blessing for us in the arms of the Father, who takes him down from the tree and wraps him in his humble love.

"He wrapped him in a linen cloth." This is an action charged with love, with tenderness, one traditionally undertaken by women, not by a man. Yet there are women here; but they do nothing! Through Joseph, the Father is revealed to us as a maternal Father, a Father of infinite tenderness.

"He laid him in a tomb." The expression here uses a verb which in Greek is thought of as a verb of motion, which would require that the verb complement be an accusative; this is the case, for example, with Joshua who was "laid in a tomb" (Josh 24:30). But here, Mark replaces the accusative with a dative as though this were not a verb of motion, suggesting that he wished to present the action as taking place very slowly, almost as if arrested, in slow motion, with great care and gentleness. Such is the Father in his invariable and eternal love for the Son.

"He rolled a stone." On Easter morning the women discover that this same stone "had been rolled away," in the opposite direction, without it being stated who had done the rolling. The young man who welcomed the women says nothing. Could it have been him? Wouldn't it be the one whose name Mark dares not pronounce, whom he is content to indicate by the turn of phrase known as the "divine passive"? "Lifting their eyes they saw that the stone had been rolled away," Mark writes (16:4), leaving it as a mystery that implies the activity of God. The one who came to roll away the stone on Easter morning had no doubt rolled it there in the first place, in the person of Joseph on the evening of the burial.

Joseph is so little in view that Mark guards against telling us anything that might indicate his thoughts, his feelings—his sadness, his love, whatever they might be. In this way Joseph is effaced as someone of whom there is nothing we can say; who, in fact, could ever say what the Father feels during the descent from the cross and the burial? Who can state the inexpressible love of the Father for the Son? The veil of the temple was split from the top to the bottom. No human words can say anything more about the Father's grief. The women, unmoving, watch in silence the one whose silence is that of measureless love.

The fact that the man from Arimathea is called Joseph is also rich enough in its implications to attract our attention, and more so when we realize that the women who watch the burial both bear the same name, Mary! When Jesus, at the beginning of his life, was laid in a crib, Mary and Joseph were there to care for him and ponder the mystery of the child; now, at the end of his life, when he is laid in a tomb, he is the object of Joseph's care and Mary's contemplation! The first Joseph who assumed the role of father, making visible the presence of the invisible Father, is now followed by another Joseph who makes visible anew the presence of the invisible Father.

After rolling across the stone, Joseph stays there, silent. The women still don't move, watching in silence. We should doubtless do the same, remaining silent, watching, immersed in mystery and without moving away from Golgotha. This, I believe, is Mark's invitation, always made in the finest of ways.

In fact, when we compare his account with those of Matthew and Luke, a constant appears. Matthew concludes his account by telling us with regard to Joseph that he "went his way" (27:60). Luke, for his part, tells us of the women that "they returned to the city" (23:56). Mark says nothing like this; no one leaves, neither Joseph nor the women. Mark has lifted his pen and watches with us! Heaven and earth are silent.

The silent Father makes no move away from his Son . . .

Measureless love!

# CHAPTER 9

# In the Dust of Death

THE WOMEN ARE THERE, silent and as if prevented from leaving. They had "followed and served Christ in Galilee, and gone up with him to Jerusalem," Mark tells us (15:41). They had followed him along the way to his cross, and we are rather like them; we too are silent, as if prevented from leaving Golgotha.

## "My God, my God, why have you forsaken me?" _____

If the women didn't leave, in addition to the reason we have already discussed, it is no doubt because during the long hours they passed at Golgotha—a short distance from the cross, at the close of the deep silence which invaded the earth along with the darkness—they heard a great cry "in a loud voice." This powerful cry uttered from the cross was a cry to split heaven and break hearts, a cry with words that could only hurt, distress and wound the women to the depths of their souls: "My God, my God, why have you forsaken me?" (15:34) The women received this cry into their hearts, this question launched towards heaven, and they were silent, awaiting the answer. But there was none! The Son was dead shortly afterwards and heaven remained mute. The silence of God exacerbated their grief. If the women watched in silence, it must be their watching reveals a profound wound which they were unable to close. Perhaps this is why they didn't move away.

Neither can we walk away from Golgotha with this unclosed wound in the heart; a wounded grief caused by the cry of the Son and the Father's failure to reply. This cry without response still resonates within us and leaves an open sore.

Only Matthew (27:46) and Mark (15:34) report this cry of Jesus. We will take time to examine their accounts the better to understand the events of Golgotha.

## The Final Temptation

"Why have you abandoned me?" It is from the pit of men's hell that the crucified man launches such a cry towards God, from the hell of mockery, calumnies and cursings, the hell of false witnesses and an unjust trial, the hell of whipping, slaps and spitting, of denial and betrayal when the cock crowed, all driven like nails into the heart. The way of the cross had been for Christ a slow descent into hell.

At the core of this human hell, amidst the mockeries heard at the foot of the cross there is one on which we need to dwell because it indicates the way this hell is deeper than might appear. Matthew, in particular, takes pains to show us that in the darkness of Golgotha, the prince of darkness came to subtly and stealthily insinuate himself, This hell is beyond the merely human, and we are dealing with a hell truly issuing from the kingdom of darkness.

It is easier in Matthew than in Mark to see the Tempter's presence, because Matthew (4:1–11), as opposed to Mark (1:12–13), reports the exact nature of the temptations given Jesus by the Tempter in the wilderness following his baptism.

Among the words heard at the foot of the cross, there was just one thing addressed directly and familiarly to Jesus as if to enter a dialogue with him: "If you are the Son of God, come down from the cross" (Matt 27:40). These words echo those he heard in the wilderness. "If you are the Son of God," the Tempter had said, "command these stones to become bread" (Matt 4:3); and again, "If you are the Son of God, throw yourself down from the temple" (4:6). What does he now say to Jesus at Golgotha? "If you are the Son of God, come down from the cross." The way he turns this phrase is exactly that of the wilderness temptations, which causes Jesus, as it does us, to realize that in the person of the casual observers at Golgotha who are speaking like this, it is the Tempter himself who is speaking, proposing a final temptation in a final effort to enter a dialogue with Christ.

To underline that these words are indeed those of the Tempter, Matthew carefully introduces what is said with a meaningful word, the word "blaspheme" (or curse). "The passers-by," Matthew writes, "cursed, saying, 'If you are the Son of God . . .'" Cursing is always drawn from the Enemy's weaponry to destroy relationship with God; cursing has its source in Satan's heart.

How did the Crucified One react? In the wilderness, Jesus responded to each of the three temptations by putting forward a verse from the Scriptures, more precisely, a verse from the Law, from the Pentateuch—Deut 6:13, 16; 8:3! In proceeding like this, Jesus was acting in a most humble way. He didn't wish to fight alone, but each time he leaned on the authority of God, his Father; each time he sought refuge in his Father's word, and at the same time he was drawing upon the power of the Holy Spirit, the one who inspired the Scriptures. What is so admirable in his way of combating the Adversary is that he did not conduct the battle alone, but together with the Father and the Holy Spirit in the indivisible union of the Trinity. Having said this, we need to be clear that the final objective of the Divider is simply to divide the Trinity. This crazy pride runs headlong into God's humility, a humility evidenced by the Son as he shelters behind the Scriptures, behind his Father's Word, given by inspiration of the Holy Spirit.

That is how Christ conducted himself in the wilderness. What will he do now at Golgotha? He does the same thing! This time he does not draw on the Pentateuch but the Psalms, which changes things a little. Effectively, the Law in the Pentateuch is the word of God as inspired by the Spirit; the psalms were also inspired by the Spirit, but nevertheless not spoken by God but addressed to him. This a little different, but the unity of the Trinity is maintained when the Son addresses the Father with a psalm inspired by the Holy Spirit.

This is how Jesus reacts at Golgotha; to be more exact, he does so by praying Psalm 22: "My God, my God, why have you forsaken me?" The Tempter will stumble against this prayer, spoken as it is in the indestructible communion of the Father, the Son and the Holy Spirit. It is a vulnerable unity because it can think in terms of an abandonment, but it is a unity all the same, since the question is posed and pronounced by the Son, received from the Holy Spirit and turned towards the Father, who alone can give the expected reply.

## The Bond of Prayer

We now need to underscore one point. In the wilderness Jesus was at pains to reply directly to each of the Adversary's temptations, replying with both finesse and address, and without falling into the traps laid. On this occasion he does not respond directly, which, in the end, is even better. The Divider's objective is to sever the bonds with God, to take for himself what belongs to God. The best way for him to break the connection is to put an end to prayer because it is prayer that forms the deep attachment to God; to cease from prayer is to break relationship with God. In hell nobody prays (Ps 6:5); there is a silence, void of any prayer (Ps 115:17). Here, at Golgotha, faced with the power of darkness which seeks to separate him from God, Jesus prays. He pays no attention to what the Tempter says; he doesn't even reply. He gives no place to the suggestion of coming down from the cross; he said "yes" to his Father to drinking the cup he was proffered, and would drink it down to the dregs without ever breaking the bond of prayer. He would reach the very end of obedience to his Father. He thus turns his back on the Tempter; he doesn't even bother to speak to him and instead prays. As with Matthew, so too with Mark: Jesus is nothing but prayer! The only words he speaks on the cross are in prayer, spoken to God.

Whereas in hell no one prays, Jesus, from the depths of the hell of Golgotha, causes his prayer to rise towards God. This—if it was all there was to it—is wonderful in itself. Not only does he pray, he shouts his prayer; he "cried with a loud voice," as Matthew (27:46) and Mark (15:34) alike tell us. From the depths of hell, Jesus addresses his prayer to God with a power that he knows to be greater than the power of darkness.

Not only this, but as he prays he says, "My God." This "my God," with the possessive pronoun, is a bond of love, a bond of trust, a bond of hope which ties him to God. To ask a question of God is to retain the bond with him and means that we expect an answer. In the depths of hell, Jesus prays, and the fact of prayer is a way of turning the back on the Divider and saying to him "No!" in a loud voice, with sovereign authority. Reader friend, it is true that to our eyes, the Crucified One appears to demonstrate great weakness; but this weakness is in humble obedience to the Father. In this weakness, Paul tells us, there shines divine power (2 Cor 12:9).

## In the Wilderness of Prayer

Darkness had now filled the earth for three hours. In these three hours of silence in the depths of hell, Jesus discovers that it is not only he who is in hell, but that so too are all those around him. All are in the same darkness since all have ceased to pray; Matthew and Mark, it seems to me, are at pains to make us aware of this. How so?

The two evangelists emphasize that, from the time on the Mount of Olives, Jesus was alone in maintaining his prayer connection with God. In Gethsemane he alone prayed while all the disciples were asleep. We have seen how Luke, for his part, portrays Gethsemane as a place of intense combat (*agōnia*), with Jesus the victor over the tempter. By contrast, Matthew and Mark are drawn instead to showing us the tempter's defeat of the disciples, a defeat the Adversary inflicts with astonishing ease. They were all asleep! Matthew explains their sleep with an important word; "their eyes," he says, "were heavy" (*bareō* 26.43). Mark exaggerates this by choosing a word with a prefix which makes it even stronger; "their eyes were super-heavy" (*katabarunō*, 14.40). Neither of them, however, state what power it was that so constrained the disciples to sleep, but it is clear that such sleep was not natural. How is that men in the prime of their lives were unable to resist sleep on the evening when the life of their master was endangered? It seems obvious to me; Satan subtly wrought this effect upon them, despite Christ's exhortation to "watch and pray, that you enter not into temptation."

The Enemy had so well manipulated Jesus' entourage that all along the way of the cross, little by little, prayer was evaporating. Peter failed to pray as he stood by the fire in the courtyard of the high priest. During the trial before the Sanhedrin, the chief priests, the scribes and the elders, all the religious leaders were no better; they didn't pray. At Golgotha, who was still praying there? Who was there when the earth was suddenly covered in darkness? The Adversary had spread his power of darkness over the whole earth.

## The Paradoxical Darkness

You will no doubt be most surprised to see the way I am now speaking of the darkness of Golgotha, when I have previously described it as the darkness of the Holy of Holies. Please do not think of this as a contradiction; it is not such, but a paradox. The darkness is paradoxical, exactly as was the thick cloud of the Exodus, when Israel left Egypt (14:20). The cloud was light on one side and darkness on the other; light on the side of liberty and life, darkness on the side of slavery and death. The darkness of Golgotha is of the same order; at the same time both that of the Holy of Holies and that of hell. The Crucified One stands at the turning point of the two; at once in the sanctuary, where he stays to speak to God the prayer of atonement, "Father, forgive them, they know not what they do," and in hell where he descends to cry from the depths, "My God, my God, why have you forsaken me?" He is fully present in both the sanctuary, watched by those who pray, and in hell where he goes to seek those who have ceased to pray.

## The Shepherd of the Lost Sheep

After his baptism in the Jordan, Jesus experienced the temptations in the wilderness; now, in the hell of Golgotha, he experiences another wilderness, a place devoid of prayer. When Zacharias, John the Baptist's father, was alone in the sanctuary all the people outside were in prayer. Luke specifies indeed that "the multitude of people were praying" (Luke 1:10). The prayer of the multitude held Zacharias up; although alone, he felt and knew himself to be sustained in this way. The prayer of others is a reality that can be felt. On the cross, in the darkness spread over the earth, Jesus feels a void of prayer around him. The silence of Golgotha between the sixth and the ninth hours is just that silence—the silence of hearts that no longer pray, that have renounced prayer, that no longer believe in prayer, that think it is foolish to pray, because God has abandoned the earth and its inhabitants. The weight of three hours of darkness is what causes Jesus to cry out; it is the weight of a darkness devoid of prayer. Jesus is there, at the center of the people; he is the shepherd in the midst of the sheep who are lost in their loss of prayer—so lost that they no longer even call out to the shepherd.

Surrounded by these lost sheep the shepherd is overcome with compassion to the core of his being (see Mark 6:34); this is why he has come, this is why his Father had sent him, to gather the sheep the wolf had scattered, for the sheep who believe themselves abandoned by

God. Jesus looks fixedly at his sheep who are lost; he feels the prayer-less void in the silence of darkness. Yes, indeed, it is for these sheep that he has come to give his life (John 10:11).

Now, face to face with the approaching wolf, the good shepherd shows his sheep the way out of hell. He has come to seek them in the deepest pit of hell, and now opens the door of salvation to them, the door of prayer. This is why "he cried out with a loud voice," so that all his sheep may recognize his voice, that they may hear him pray, and that they might hear his prayer as an invitation to pray themselves, to pray with him this prayer in which it is surely so easy to join: "My God, my God, why have you forsaken me?"

## The Prayer of the Forsaken

When Jesus joins his sheep in the silence of hell he doesn't give them his own prayer, but theirs. We note that when Jesus prays in the gospels, he always speaks to God as "Father," never "My God." Here, however, for the first time, he prays differently; he could have expressed his suffering in his own words, but, no! He speaks a prayer belonging to his people, in fellowship with all the forsaken ones, all who feel forsaken. In his humble love, he divests himself of his own prayer, his habitual prayer to the Father, humbly adopting the prayer of his sheep, their way of praying "my God," as was their custom. Jesus chooses for them the prayer which best suits their needs, the prayer of Psalm 22, the prayer of those who feel, believe and think themselves abandoned by God, rejected, deserted and excluded, damned in the darkness of hell. Jesus the shepherd comes to save the lost sheep, opening to them the door of prayer. He prays with them, in the midst of them, like them and for them. In order to be closer to them, he doesn't speak the psalm in Hebrew, the language of God's chosen, but in Aramean, the language of the poor and unimportant who believe themselves deserted by him: "Eli, Eli, lama sabaktani." This is the tenderness of a shepherd for his lost sheep.

Jesus demonstrates to us that in the pit of hell, in hell's silence, there is still a place for prayer. To pray Psalm 22 with him, to follow him step by step, verse by verse along the pathway of prayer which leads to God, the path which provides a way of return to God, this is what Jesus invites us to do in the depths of our hell. In praying this psalm, Jesus takes upon his shoulders the lost sheep and carries them in his prayer. Jesus gives his life by giving us prayer. He dies seeking after his sheep, not in becoming lost with them. To love his sheep does not mean becoming a sheep and being lost with them. To love his sheep means being always the shepherd and opening the doorway of prayer as a rupture in hell's walls.

## The Liar's Ruse

"My God, my God, why have you forsaken me?" The doorway is now open but the darkness is still there, powerfully opposing its force of deceit to the vulnerability of prayer's truth. The power of deceit is to continue have us believing the God doesn't hear, doesn't answer and that prayer is in vain. The Liar's ruse is to rely on the silence which followed Jesus' prayer as evidencing heaven's silence, the absence of any response and the absence of God; Jesus, however, knows that God's response is given, but in a different and very surprising way, given in fact by God in Psalm 22 itself at the heart of the psalm. To understand this, it is enough to pray the psalm with him, right through to its end. On the cross he prays the opening of the psalm with the objective of praying it through in its entirety in fellowship with us, expecting that we would indeed follow it to its end. To believe that Jesus is the good shepherd means following him in this psalm, verse by verse, to pray it right through with him—it is where God's answer is found.

Jesus dies opening the door of prayer. Had he spoken the truth? Yes indeed, as the women who looked on could all well attest, because of what happened immediately after his death. The veil of the temple was rent "from top to bottom" (Matt 27:51; Mark 15:3), ripped by God himself, thus opening in style the door of prayer, the door to the Holy of Holies, the door that leads into the darkness of the Holy of Holies, into the presence of God whose arms are open wide in welcome to those who tread the pathway of prayer with Christ.

The torn veil was a sign for the people, and a much-awaited response from God—a sign given as encouragement, an invitation to pursue prayer, to persevere in it. The Son opened the door of prayer, and the Father flings it wide, forever rending the veil that blocked the way to his Father's heart. This is God's response to the people, given to those Christ gathered together in his prayer; this response is a wonderful blessing.

We need to be attentive here! This response was certainly received by the people, but not by Jesus, who was unable to receive it. According to the gospels of Matthew and Mark, Jesus died before the veil was torn; he didn't hear it. Instead, he only heard further mockery, the lie that would have him believe no one would answer, not even Elijah; the lies and the spite of giving him vinegar. Nevertheless, we can surely believe that through these last mockeries, to which he would have paid no attention, Jesus continued his praying of Psalm 22 to its conclusion, hearing and welcoming in it his Father's response.

## Right to the End of the Psalm

The women received the ripping of the veil as an encouragement given by the Father to pursue the way of prayer opened by the Son. The psalm is a magnificent gift from the shepherd to his sheep; like all the psalms, it is also a gift from the Holy Spirit, with the psalmist as intermediary. To pray it is to abandon oneself in trust to the Holy

Spirit; it is also the very pathway followed by Christ before his death as he abandoned himself to the Holy Spirit to be led to the Father. This is how the Son died, in prayer in communion with the Holy Spirit, who leads to the Father. What marvelous unity in the Trinity, which the Divider cannot touch.

The women are there, and so are we, when this psalm is cried out from the cross by the Son and deposited by him in our hearts for the Holy Spirit to pray with us and lead us to the Father. The Trinity is revealed to us, welcoming us into the heart of the mystery of God.

Before we leave Golgotha, reader friend, it remains for us to pray through the psalm with the women, with Christ and with the Holy Spirit. We now have only this much more to do, and we do it in obedience to Christ, who has given his life opening the doorway of the psalms. First, however, we should look at the way the evangelists themselves meditated this psalm long before us, as they prepared the accounts they offer us of Christ's crucifixion.

## The Psalm Prayed by the Evangelists

According to the custom in Israel, in quoting the opening words of a scriptural text, reference is made to the entire text. If one quotes the opening of a psalm, as Jesus does on the cross, it is because the whole psalm is being treasured in the heart as an interior prayer one is appropriating. The evangelists knew this and understand that when Jesus quoted the opening of Psalm 22, he was praying it in its totality at the moment he died. For them, the psalm therefore took on such importance that they prayed and meditated it before editing their accounts of the crucifixion; we can confirm this as we read and note the numerous references and allusions to it. An inexpressible light mysteriously shines in the psalm; it pierces the darkness around and illuminates Golgotha in an extraordinary way. The four evangelists searched diligently for clues and illuminate their descriptions with the light they found.

We can begin with Mark, since that has been our starting place in this chapter. This is how he opens his account of the crucifixion: "they crucified him and parted his garments, casting lots to see what each should take" (15:24). Luke, as we have seen, begins his account with Jesus' prayer, a lovely way to start. John describes the inscription which spoke of Jesus as king (19:18–22), which is also very lovely. But Matthew, like Mark, begins with the dividing of the garments, and this is surprising. Why focus on this highly sordid event? The reason is that the parting of the clothing has great importance, announced as it is in Psalm 22, where we read, "they part my garments and cast lots for my tunic" (v. 18). We can sense in Mark a certain restrained jubilation; what the Holy Spirit announced at the time of the psalmist is actually being experienced by the Son.

This is not all, however. If this incident announced by the Holy Spirit is actually taking place at Golgotha, it also indicates that the Father is present and attentive to the accomplishment of the Scriptures.

Everything that can be said about the parting of the garments can also be said about another detail thrown into relief by Mark, one which concerns the passers-by. He tells us that they "shook their heads" (15:29),[1] an action which the psalm makes clear is another fulfilled prediction: "all those who see me wag their head" (Ps 22:7).

Matthew does exactly the same as Mark; he stops on the same points, on the same verses from the psalm, but adds another allusion in a similar vein to Mark. Matthew reports the comments of religious leaders as they mock Jesus in the following terms, "Let God deliver him if he delights in him" (27:43), which is a clear reference to the psalm, "Let him deliver him seeing he delighted in him" (v. 8).

Neither Luke nor John record the cry of Psalm 22 from Jesus' mouth, but both, nevertheless, pondered this psalm, and it helped them produce their accounts. Both refer to the parting of the garments and John indeed specifies that it was a fulfilment of the scriptures (19:24; Luke 23:34). For his part, Luke retains a word which is very rare in the

1. "wagged" KJV. (Trans.)

Old Testament but which is found in the psalm (v. 7) to describe the attitude of the rulers who "held Jesus in derision" (*ekmuktērizō*, 23:35).

With regard to John, he may perhaps have been alluding to verse 15 of Psalm 22 when he reports Jesus' words, "I thirst" (19:28).

By writing in the way they do, the four evangelists demonstrate that meditation drawing on Psalm 22 is a pathway of light opened up by the Holy Spirit. The meditation illumines the profound mystery of the cross as well as the psalm itself.

## The Psalm Prayed by Jesus

We have seen evidence of the four evangelists contemplating Psalm 22, pondering the crucifixion in the light of the psalm; it remains for us too, I believe, to meditate it, endeavoring to perceive how Jesus himself would have experienced the psalm which was in a way his final prayer. Our part is to open wide the door to our heart in the hope of perceiving if possible the Father's response, to understand and ponder it. If God was concerned with the fulfilment of the verses about the garments and the "wagging" of the head, he would surely also be concerned with the fulfilment of all the psalm reveals of his humble and measureless love for his Son. When the Holy Spirit led the Son to pray this psalm from the cross, would that not also be so that he taste the humble and measureless love it reveals, in which he is enveloped until his final breath?

To hear the Father's voice in the psalm seems difficult; it might even be impossible, given that the psalm is a lengthy monologue which records no word from God. In fact, the psalm shows us attitudes and silent actions on God's part, which we can indeed consider. In his long monologue, the psalmist describes his experience at God's hand, not only what he had been through in the past but what he is experiencing in the present. It is here, in Christ's present experience, that we suddenly discover, in the light of the Holy Spirit, an action of the Father's;

it is an overwhelming action, which magnificently reveals the measureless and humble love of the Father for the Son. In this silent action, we realize that the grievous cry of the Son, "My God, my God, why have you forsaken me?" receives a silent response from his Father, a wonderful response which plunges us into the silence of contemplation.

Here is what the psalmist says, and what Christ experiences in making the psalm his own; it is what the Son says to the Father, praying the psalm from the pit of hell: "my heart is like wax; it is melted within me. My strength is dried up like broken shards of pottery and my tongue sticks to the roof of my mouth" (vv. 14–15), and then this overwhelming statement, "You have laid me in the dust of death."

"You have laid me in the dust of death." What an extraordinary action. A silent action of the Father on the Son's behalf in the depths of hell. This is the content of the Father's silence at the heart of the darkness, this is his response to his Son's cry. In silence, he accompanies his Son into the depths of hell, descends with him, carrying him in his arms into the dust of death, there to lay him down. The infinite love of the Father, who himself goes down into hell with his Son, without leaving him for an instant; humble love which goes this far, to this silent, extreme act of fathomless tenderness.

The verse is overwhelming; it makes us realize that Jesus spoke the psalm within the arms of his Father, "on the bosom of his Father," as his well-beloved disciple would write (John 1:18). He who is on the bosom of his Father from all eternity is still there, even at the hour of death. What a wonder it is for us to discover that nothing has been able to separate the Father from the Son in their humble love; nothing, not even the darkness of hell, nor the power of the Prince of darkness. The Divider is unable to divide the humble love of the Father and the Son.

Christ dies declaring this psalm to his Father, who silently clasps him in his arms. As we listen to him speak, we realize that he is speaking to the Father as the living speak to the living. He who is truly dead in the hands of men is truly alive in the arms of his Father. Death, which is sovereign in the kingdom of hell, is now simply and magnificently vanquished by humble divine love.

The fathomless mystery of love!

Humble Son, you who, in love,
had no fear of making yourself obedient
to the very point of death on the cross,
how blessed you are!

Humble Holy Spirit, you who, in love,
placed this psalm in the mouth
and in the heart of the Son,
how blessed you are!

Humble Father, you who, in love,
had no fear of going down with your Son
into the very impurity of hell,
how blessed you are!

Praises to you, Holy Trinity,
you, who in humble love,
have vanquished death
your final enemy!

Holy Trinity, we adore you!